HARCOURT SCIENCE

WORKBOOK

Harcourt School Publishers

Orlando • Boston • Dallas • Chicago • San Diego

www.harcourtschool.com

Copyright © by Harcourt, Inc.

All rights reserved. No part of this publication may be reproduced or transmitted in any form or by any means, electronic or mechanical, including photocopy, recording, or any information storage and retrieval system, without permission in writing from the publisher.

Permission is hereby granted to individual teachers using the corresponding student's textbook or kit as the major vehicle for regular classroom instruction to photocopy complete pages from this publication in classroom quantities for instructional use and not for resale. Requests for information on other matters regarding duplication of this work should be addressed to School Permissions and Copyrights, Harcourt, Inc., 6277 Sea Harbor Drive, Orlando, Florida 32887-6777. Fax: 407-345-2418.

HARCOURT and the Harcourt Logo are trademarks of Harcourt, Inc., registered in the United States of America and/or other jurisdictions.

Printed in the United States of America

ISBN 0-15-323711-2

10 022 10 09 08 07 06

Contents

UNIT A — Plants and Animals All Around

Chapter 1—Living and Nonliving Things   WB1–WB8

Chapter 2—All About Plants   WB9–WB18

Chapter 3—All About Animals   WB19–WB34

UNIT B — Living Together

Chapter 1—Plants and Animals Need One Another   WB35–WB44

Chapter 2—A Place to Live   WB45–WB56

UNIT C — About Our Earth

Chapter 1—Earth's Land   WB57–WB66

Chapter 2—Our Natural Resources   WB67–WB78

UNIT D — Weather, the Sky, and Seasons

Chapter 1—Measuring Weather......................WB79–WB90

Chapter 2—The Sky and the Seasons............WB91–WB106

UNIT E — Matter and Energy

Chapter 1—Investigate Matter........................WB107–WB122

Chapter 2—Making Sound..............................WB123–WB132

UNIT F — Forces

Chapter 1—Pushes and Pulls........................WB133–WB146

Chapter 2—Magnets.......................................WB147–WB158

Introduction to Unit Experiments.................WB159–WB162

Unit A Experiment...WB163–WB165

Unit B Experiment...WB166–WB168

Unit C Experiment...WB169–WB171

Unit D Experiment...WB172–WB174

Unit E Experiment...WB175–WB177

Unit F Experiment...WB178–WB180

How Scientists Work

Science Safety

Think ahead.

Be neat and clean.

Be careful.

Do not eat or drink things.

Safety Symbols

Be careful!

Sharp!

Be careful!

Wear an apron.

Wear goggles.

Science Safety

____ I will think ahead.

____ I will read the directions and follow them.

____ I will be neat with my materials.

____ I will take care of all science supplies.

____ I will clean up when I am done.

____ I will return all unused materials to my teacher.

____ I will be careful. I will follow all of the cautions.

____ I will not taste things I am using in an investigation unless my teacher tells me to.

Name _____

Unit A, Chapter 1 Living and Nonliving

LESSON 2
What Are Living and Nonliving Things?

1. Living things need ____, water, and ____.

2. Animals, plants, and people are ____.

3. Nonliving things do not need food, ____, or ____.

4. Nonliving things do not ____.

LESSON 1
How Do My Senses Help Me Learn?

My 5 senses are

1. _____
2. _____
3. _____
4. _____
5. _____

Use with page A3.

WB1 • Workbook

Name _____

Observe

Draw a line to the sense each person is using.

1. touch •
2. taste •
3. hear •
4. see •
5. smell •

6. Circle all the senses the boy can use to find out about the banana.

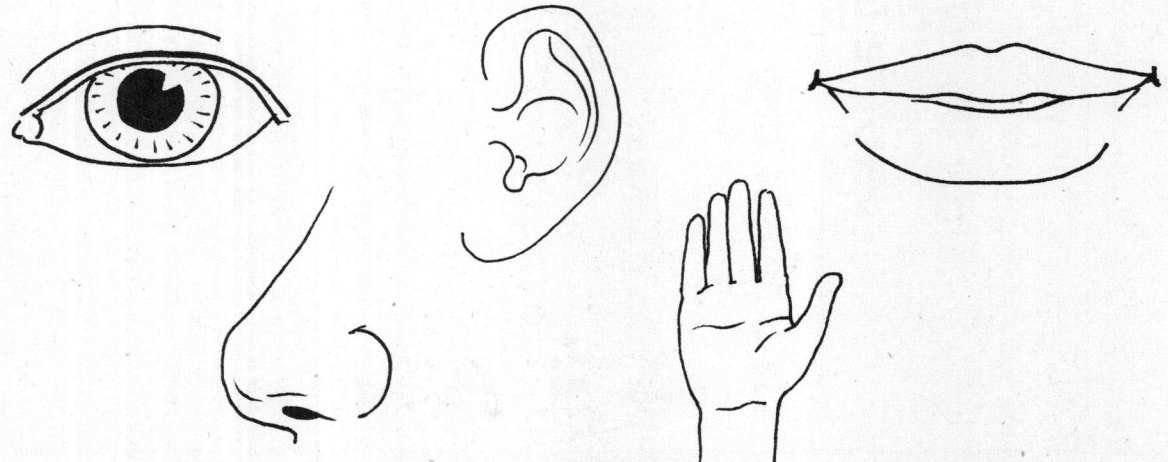

WB2 • Workbook   Use with page A4.

Name _____

How Do My Senses Help Me Learn?

Match the body part to the sense.

1. sight •

2. hearing •

3. smell •

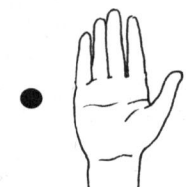

4. touch •

5. taste •

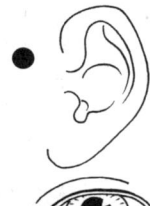

6. Circle all the senses the boy is using.

Use with page A9.

Name _____

Compare

1. Tell how the baby and the doll are the same.
_____
_____
_____
_____

2. Tell how the baby and the doll are different.
_____
_____
_____
_____

Name _____

What Are Living and Nonliving Things?

Color the living things **red**.
Color the nonliving things **blue**.

1. Flowers grow. Tell one other thing in the picture that will grow.

_____
_____

2. Tell one thing in the picture that is nonliving.

_____
_____

Use with page A15.

Workbook • WB5

Name _____

Living and Nonliving Things

Write the word from the box that best completes each sentence.

| living | nonliving | senses |

1. You can use your five _____ to help you learn.

2. Plants, animals, and people are _____ _____ things.

3. Things that do not need food, water, and _____ air are _____ things.

4. Circle the word that tells about the picture.

   living   nonliving

WB6 • Workbook   Use with pages A4–A15.

Name _____

Reading Skills Practice

Sentences

Read the sentences. Draw a line under the first word of each sentence. Then draw a circle around the period in each sentence.

Senses

Your eyes can see a sunset .

Your skin can feel a furry kitten .

Your ears can hear a tapping drum .

Your nose can smell a rose .

Your mouth can taste a sour lemon .

Look at the picture. Write a sentence about the picture. Draw a line under the first word of your sentence. Then draw a circle around the period in your sentence.

_____
_____
_____

Use with page A7.

Name _____

 **Writing Practice**

Write to Describe

A. Choose one of your senses. Draw one living thing and one nonliving thing you learn about with that sense.

Sense _____

Living Thing	Nonliving Thing

B. Write about what you drew.

_____
_____
_____
_____

WB8 • Workbook   Use with pages A18–A19.

Name _____

Unit A, Chapter 2 All About Plants

LESSON 1 What Are the Parts of a Plant?	LESSON 2 How Do Plants Grow?	LESSON 3 What Do Plants Need?
The parts of a plant are 1. _____ 2. _____ 3. _____ 4. _____	1. Most plants grow from _____. 2. Plants need _____. 3. Roots grow in the _____.	Plants need 1. _____ 2. _____ 3. _____ 4. _____

Use with page A21.

Name _____

Compare

maple tree

daisy

tomato

1. Tell how the plants are the same.
_____
_____
_____
_____

2. Tell how the plants are different.
_____
_____
_____
_____
_____
_____

Name _____

What Are the Parts of a Plant?

1. Label each plant part. Use the words in the box.

| roots | stem | leaves | flower |

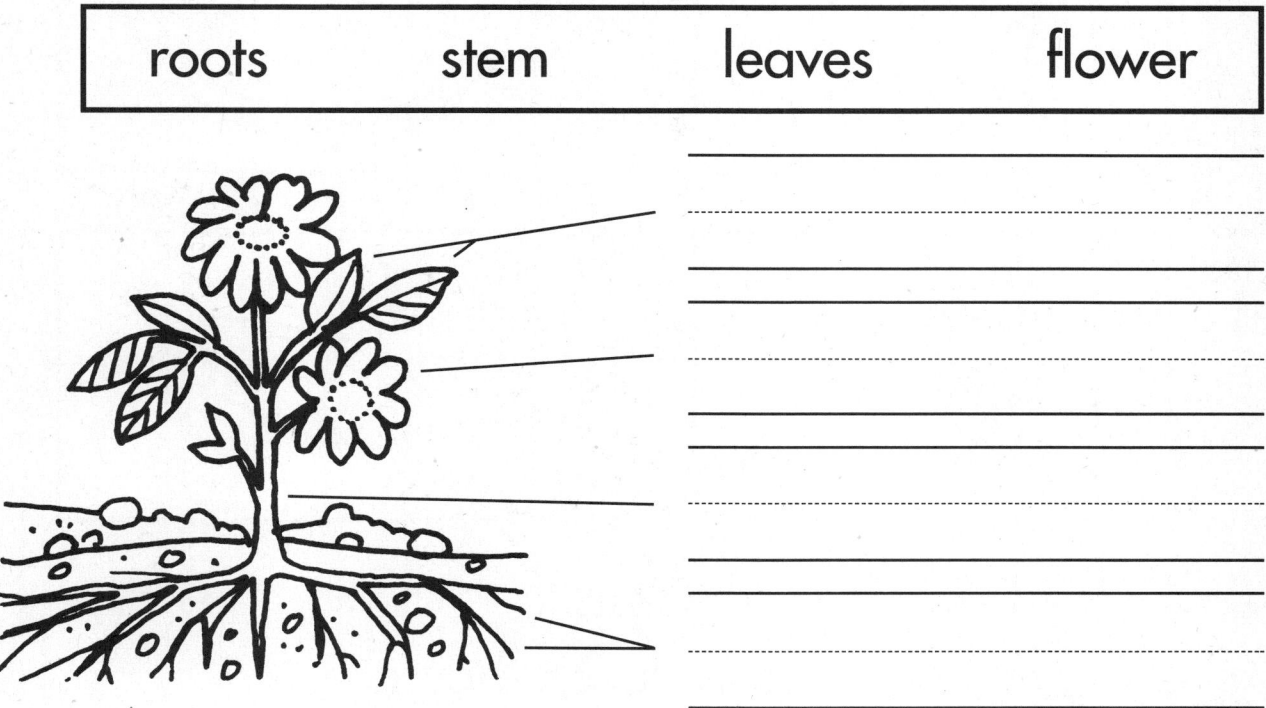

_____
_____
_____
_____
_____
_____

2. Color the plant part that makes food **green**.

3. Color the plant part that holds the plant in soil and takes in water **yellow**.

4. Color the plant part that moves water from the roots to the leaves **brown**.

5. Color the plant part that makes seeds **red**.

Use with page A27.

Workbook • WB11

Name _____

Observe

Circle the seeds in each picture.

1.

2.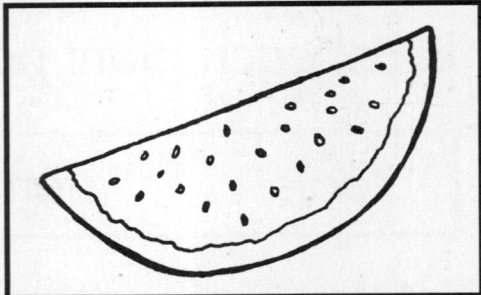

3.

4.

5. Draw two kinds of seeds.
   Write what kinds of seeds they are.

WB12 • Workbook

Use with page A28.

Name _____

How Do Plants Grow?

1. This is a flower seed. What might the plant look like when it grows?

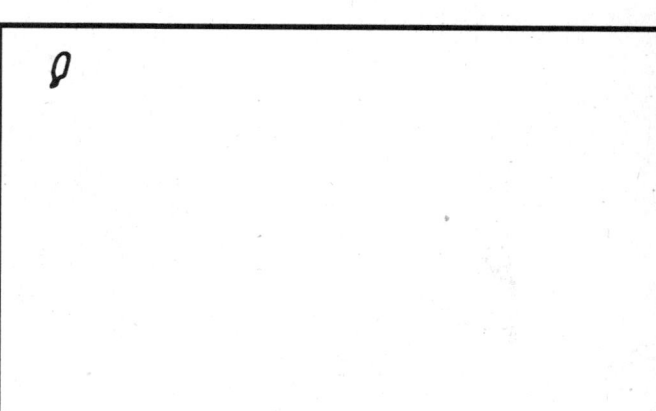

2. This is a pumpkin seed. What might the plant look like when it grows?

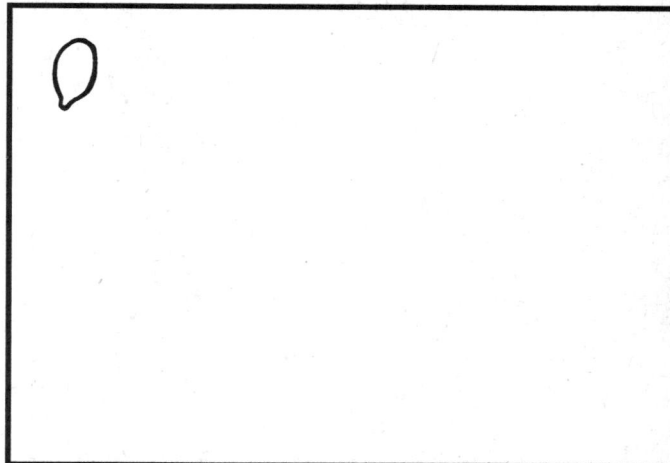

3. Color all the things that grew from seeds.

Name _____

Communicate

1. Draw and color a plant. Show a partner the different parts of your plant.

[   ]

Tell two things that all plants need. Add these things to your drawings.

2. _____ **3.** _____

WB14 • Workbook   Use with page A32.

Name _____

What Do Plants Need?

1. Plants need air to grow. Circle two other things that plants need to grow.

2. The plant near the window is growing well. The plant in the corner is **not** growing well. Tell why.

_____
_____
_____
_____

Use with page A35.   Workbook • WB15

Name _____

All About Plants

Write your answers. Use the words in the box.

| flower | leaves | roots |
| stem | seed | seed coat |

1. I hold plants in the soil. What am I?
_____
_____

2. I help hold up the plant. What am I?
_____
_____

3. I make food. What am I?
_____
_____

4. I make seeds. What am I?
_____
_____

5. Most plants grow from this.
_____
_____

WB16 • Workbook   Use with pages A22–A35.

Name _____

Headings

Read the sentences. Circle the heading that would be used with the sentences.

1. **Parts of a Plant**
   Parts of a Carrot
   How Plant Parts Help a Plant

   Plants have different parts.
   Most plants have roots, a stem, and leaves.
   Some plants have flowers.

2. Write a heading to go with the sentences and picture.

   _____

   There are different kinds of leaves.
   One of the leaves is an oak leaf.
   One of the leaves is a maple leaf.

Use with page A24. Workbook • WB17

Name _____

Write to Inform

A. On the plate, draw seeds or a food made with seeds that you like to eat.

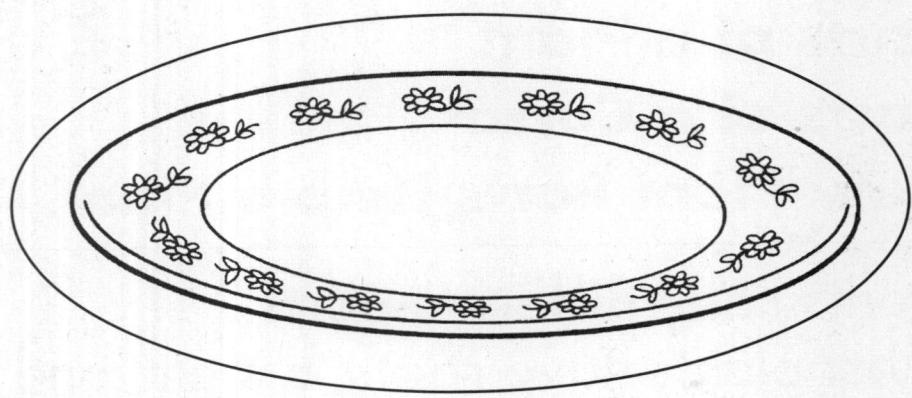

B. Write about the seeds you drew. Tell what kind of plant they would grow to be.

_____
_____
_____
_____
_____
_____
_____
_____

Name _____

Unit A, Chapter 3 All About Animals

LESSON 1 Animal Needs

Animals need

1. _____
2. _____
3. _____
4. _____

LESSON 2 Kinds of Animals

Some kinds of animals

1. _____
2. _____
3. _____
4. _____
5. _____

LESSON 3 Insects

1. Insects have __ legs and __ body parts.
2. Insects lay __.
3. Insects have strong __ coverings.

LESSON 4 Animal Growth

1. Animals grow to look like their __.
2. Some animals hatch from __.

LESSON 5 Butterfly Growth

1. A butterfly passes through __ stages.
2. Wings keep butterflies __.

LESSON 6 Frog Growth

1. A frog is an __.
2. A frog passes through __ stages.

Use with page A41.

Name _____

Observe

Each animal is meeting a need. Tell which need. Use words from the box.

| shelter | air | water | food |

1. _____

2. _____

3. _____

4. Draw an animal. Show it meeting its needs.

WB20 • Workbook

Use with page A42.

Name _____

What Do Animals Need?

1. Animals need air. Color three other things this bird needs to live.

Some animals have sharp teeth. Some have flat teeth. Match each animal to its teeth.

2.

 • •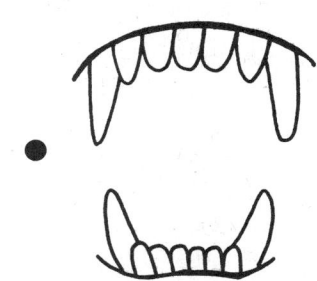

3.

 • •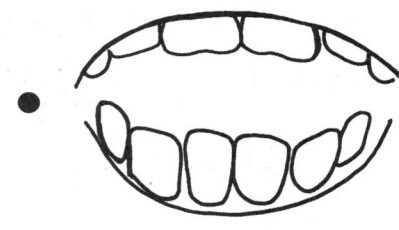

Use with page A47.

Workbook • WB21

Name _____

Classify

Match each animal to its body covering.

1. mammal •

2. bird •

3. reptile •

4. amphibian •

5. fish •

6. Write the name or draw a picture of an animal in each group.

Mammal	Bird	Reptile

_____ _____ _____

WB22 • Workbook   Use with page A48.

Name _____

What Are Some Kinds of Animals?

Many kinds of animals live in this forest.

1. Color all the amphibians **orange**.
2. Color all the mammals **brown**.
3. Color all the reptiles **green**.
4. Color all the birds **blue**.
5. Another kind of animal is also in the picture. Write its name.

_____

_____

Use with page A53.

Name _____

Make a Model

1. Draw the parts so they make an insect.

 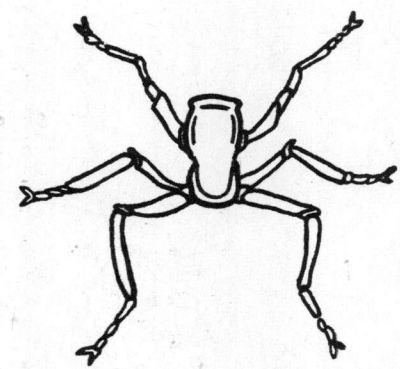 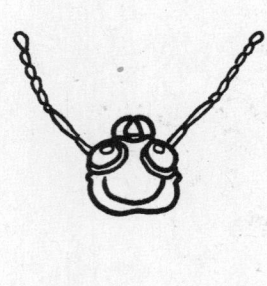

2. Name this insect.
_____
_____

WB24 • Workbook   Use with page A54.

Name _____

 Concept Review

What Are Insects?

1. Color the animals that are insects.

  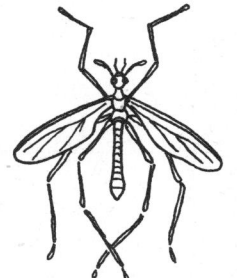

2. How many body parts does an insect have? _____

3. How many legs does an insect have? _____

4. Draw two kinds of insects. Draw one with wings.

Use with page A57.

Workbook • WB25

Name _____

Compare

1. Compare the animals.

	Ways they are the same.	**Ways they are different.**
swan		
dog		

2. Circle the part that shows how these animals are helping their young.

Name _____

Concept Review

How Do Animals Grow?

Match the animal to where it came from.

1.  •

2.  •

3.  •

4.  •

 •

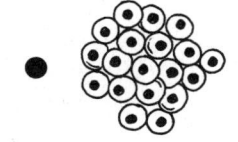 •

 •

 •

5. What are two things an animal can teach its young?

_____
_____
_____
_____

Name _____

Observe

1. Color the butterflies **red**.
2. Color the larva **blue**.
3. Color the pupa **yellow**.
4. From what does a caterpillar hatch?
_____
_____

5. What comes out of a pupa?
_____
_____

WB28 • Workbook   Use with page A64.

Name _____

How Does a Butterfly Grow?

Draw a line under the best ending.

1. A caterpillar hatches from an egg. The caterpillar becomes a pupa and makes a hard covering. The pupa changes into a ____.

    larva   butterfly   bigger caterpillar

2. These butterflies live in a field of flowers. They keep safe by hiding. Color the flowers and the butterflies. Help the butterflies hide.

Name _____

Sequence

1. Tell how the frog grows after it hatches. Write **first**, **next**, or **last** next to each picture.

_____
_____

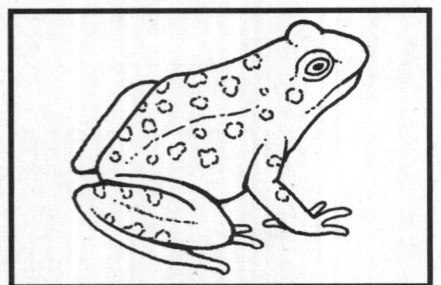

_____
_____
_____

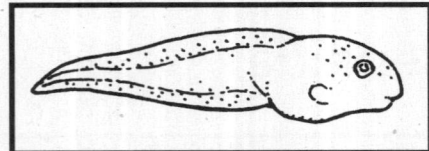

_____
_____

2. Read the sentences. Number them in sequence. The first one is done for you.

_____ Young frogs climb onto land.

_____ Tadpoles use their tails to swim.

____1____ Frogs lay eggs in the water.

_____ Tadpoles hatch from the eggs.

WB30 • Workbook Use with page A70.

Name _____

How Does a Frog Grow?

1. Finish each drawing.

       tadpole   frog

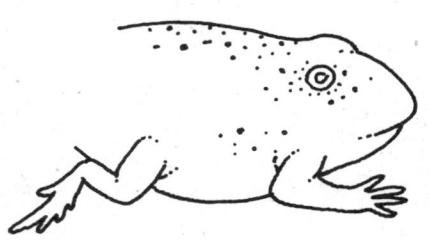 

2. What part of the tadpole helps it to swim? Color that part **red**.

3. Draw where a frog will lay its eggs.

Use with page A73.   Workbook • WB31

Name _____

All About Animals

1. What kind of animal is it? Draw a line to match.

   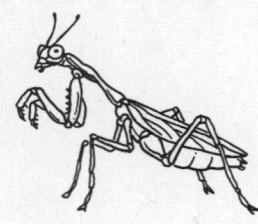

• • • •

• • • •

amphibian   insect   reptile   mammal

Finish the sentences. Use the words in the box.

| hatch | larva | pupa |

2. When chicks break out of eggs, they _____.

3. A tiny caterpillar is called a _____.

4. A caterpillar makes a hard covering called a _____.

WB32 • Workbook   Use with pages A42–A73.

Name _____

Recall Supporting Facts and Details

Read and answer the questions.

Animals and Food

Animals use their body parts to help them get the food they need. A wolf uses its sharp teeth to tear and chew meat. Cows eat grass. They use their flat teeth for chewing. Some birds use their beaks to catch fish. An eagle uses its claws to catch its food.

1. What kind of teeth is used to chew grass? _____

2. How can an eagle catch its food? _____

3. How can a bird catch a fish? _____

Use with page A44.   Workbook • WB33

Name _____

 Writing Practice

Write to Inform

A. Draw one of your favorite animals in its home.

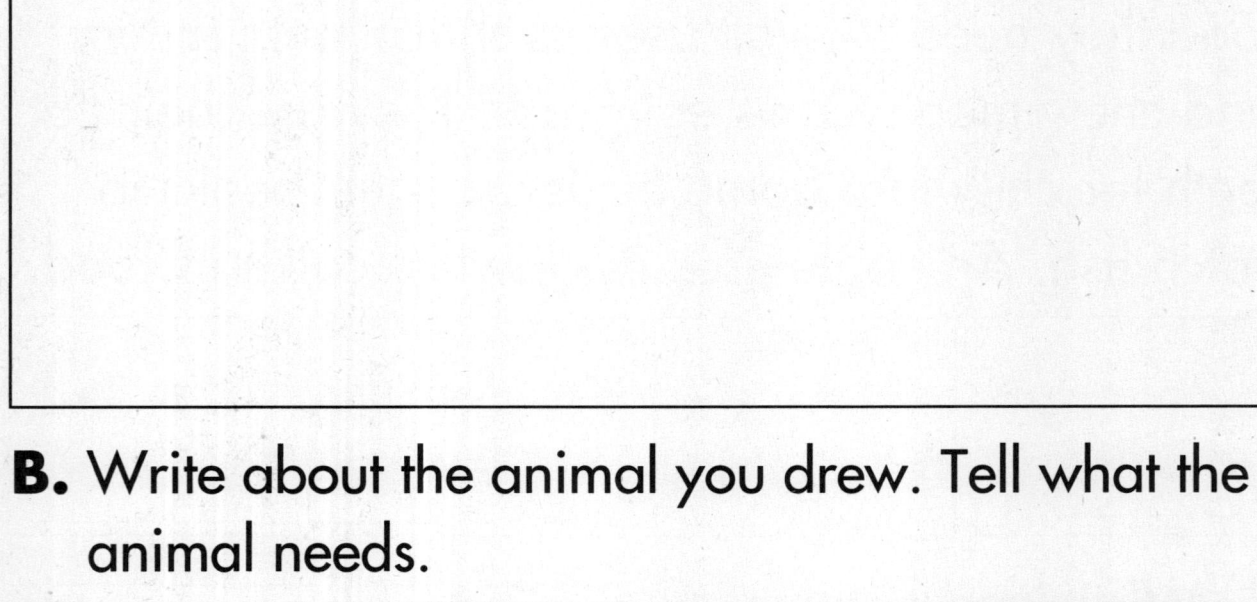

B. Write about the animal you drew. Tell what the animal needs.

_____
_____
_____
_____
_____
_____

Name _____

Unit B, Chapter 1 Plants and Animals Need One Another		
LESSON 1 **How Do Animals Need Plants?**	**LESSON 2** **How Do Animals Help Plants?**	**LESSON 3** **How Do We Need Plants and Animals?**
Animals need plants for: 1. _____. 2. _____. 3. _____ materials.	1. Animals move _____ to new places. 2. A butterfly may carry _____ from flower to flower. 3. Worms _____ the soil.	1. People need plants and animals for _____, shelter, and _____. 2. People use plants to make _____.

Use with page B3.

Workbook • WB35

Name _____

Observe

Animals use plants for different things.

1. Color the plants used for food **green**.
2. One animal uses a plant to make a nest. Color the nest **yellow**.
3. Color the plants used for shelter **brown**.
4. One animal uses plants to hide. Tell about that animal.

_____
_____
_____
_____

WB36 • Workbook   Use with page B4.

Name _____

 Concept Review

How Do Animals Need Plants?

1. Match each animal to how it is using plants.

   •   • shelter

   •   • food

2. Finish the drawing. Show how an animal uses a log for shelter and food.

Use with page B9.   Workbook • WB37

Name _____

Investigate

A plant grew in Jason's yard. A plant just like it grew in Sara's yard. Sara and Jason investigate how a seed was carried to Sara's yard.

1. Circle what you think moved the seed from one yard to the other.

2. Tell how the seed may have moved.
   _____
   _____
   _____
   _____
   _____

Name _____

How Do Animals Help Plants?

1. Circle the animals that are helping plants.

2. Tell how a butterfly helps a flower. Write or draw.

_____
_____
_____
_____
_____

Use with page B13.

Workbook • WB39

Name _____

Classify

Circle the things made from plants. Mark an **X** on the things made from animals.

1. 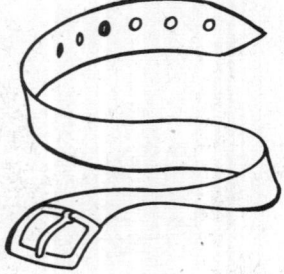   **2.** 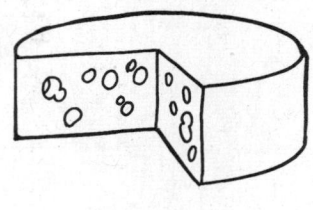   **3.**

4.    **5.** 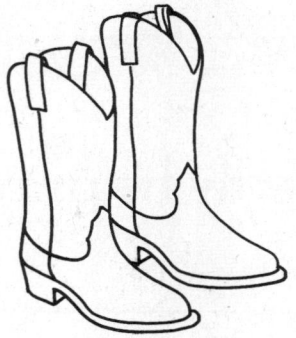   **6.**

7. 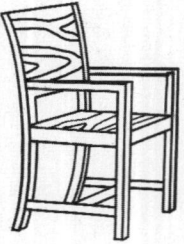   **8.** 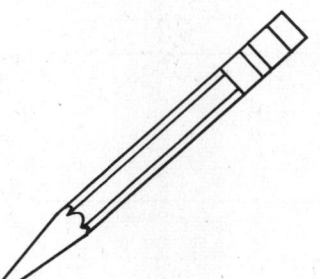   **9.**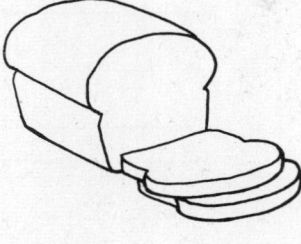

Name _____

Concept Review

How Do We Need Plants and Animals?

Match each product to the animal or plant it came from.

1.  •   •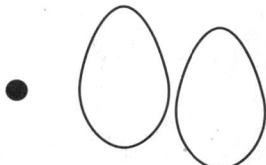

2.  •   •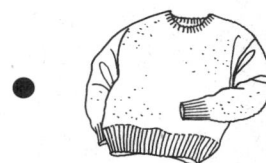

3.  •   •

4.  •   •

5. Tell how an animal can be a helper to a person. Write or draw.

_____
_____
_____

Use with page B19.

Name _____

Plants and Animals Need One Another

Draw a line under each sentence that is true.

1. Animals use shelter for food.
2. Wastes can help enrich soil.
3. Wool is an animal product used for clothing.
4. Powder from flowers is called pollen.

Match each word to the correct picture.

5. shelter •   •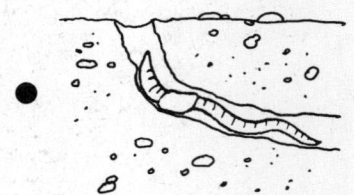

6. enrich •   •

7. product •   •

8. pollen •   •

Name _____

Reading Skills Practice

Use Context

Underline the word or words that help you know what the shaded word means.

1. The waste of a worm enriches the soil and makes the soil better for plants.

2. A cat can carry a seed and move it to a new place to grow.

Look at the pictures. Mark an **X** on the animals or insects that carry pollen from flower to flower.

Tell how an animal can carry seeds to a new place.
_____
_____
_____
_____

Use with page B12.   Workbook • WB43

Name _____

Writing Practice

Write to Persuade

A. Plan an ad for a product made from plants. Draw the product. Make up a name for your product.

[ ]

Product Name _____

B. Write a sentence telling why people should use your product.

_____
_____
_____
_____

WB44 • Workbook   Use with pages B22–B23.

Name _____

Unit B, Chapter 2 A Place to Live

LESSON 1
What Lives in a Forest?

1. A forest is _____ .
2. Plants get the _____ they need in the forest.
3. Animals find _____ and _____ in the forest.

LESSON 3
What Lives in a Rain Forest?

1. A rain forest gets a lot of _____ .
2. Plants and animals use different levels among the trees for _____ and _____ .

LESSON 2
What Lives in the Desert?

1. A desert is a _____ place. There is little _____ .
2. Desert plants hold _____ .
3. Desert animals have ways to stay _____ .

LESSON 4
What Lives in the Ocean?

1. An ocean is _____ water.
2. Ocean animals use plants for _____ and _____ .

Use with page B25.   Workbook • WB45

Name _____

Compare

1. Tell how these leaves are the same.
   _____
   _____
   _____
   _____

2. Tell how they are different.
   _____
   _____
   _____
   _____

oak

maple

3. Tell how these leaves are the same.
   _____
   _____
   _____
   _____

4. Tell how they are different.
   _____
   _____
   _____
   _____

rose

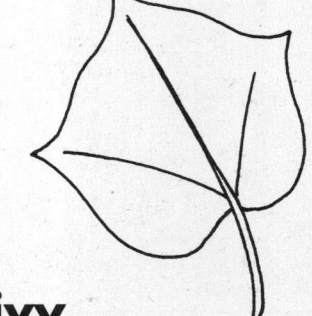
ivy

WB46 • Workbook   Use with page B26.

Name _____

What Lives in a Forest?

Answer **yes** or **no**.

1. Are there many trees in a forest? _____
2. Does the soil stay dry? _____
3. Is there a lot of sunlight on the forest floor? _____
4. Do some trees grow tall in a forest? _____
5. Finish the picture of the forest. Show plants and animals that live in a forest.

Use with page B29.

Name _____

 Science Skills Practice

Draw a Conclusion

These animals live in a desert. Put an **X** where an animal might go to stay cool in the daytime. Color the picture.

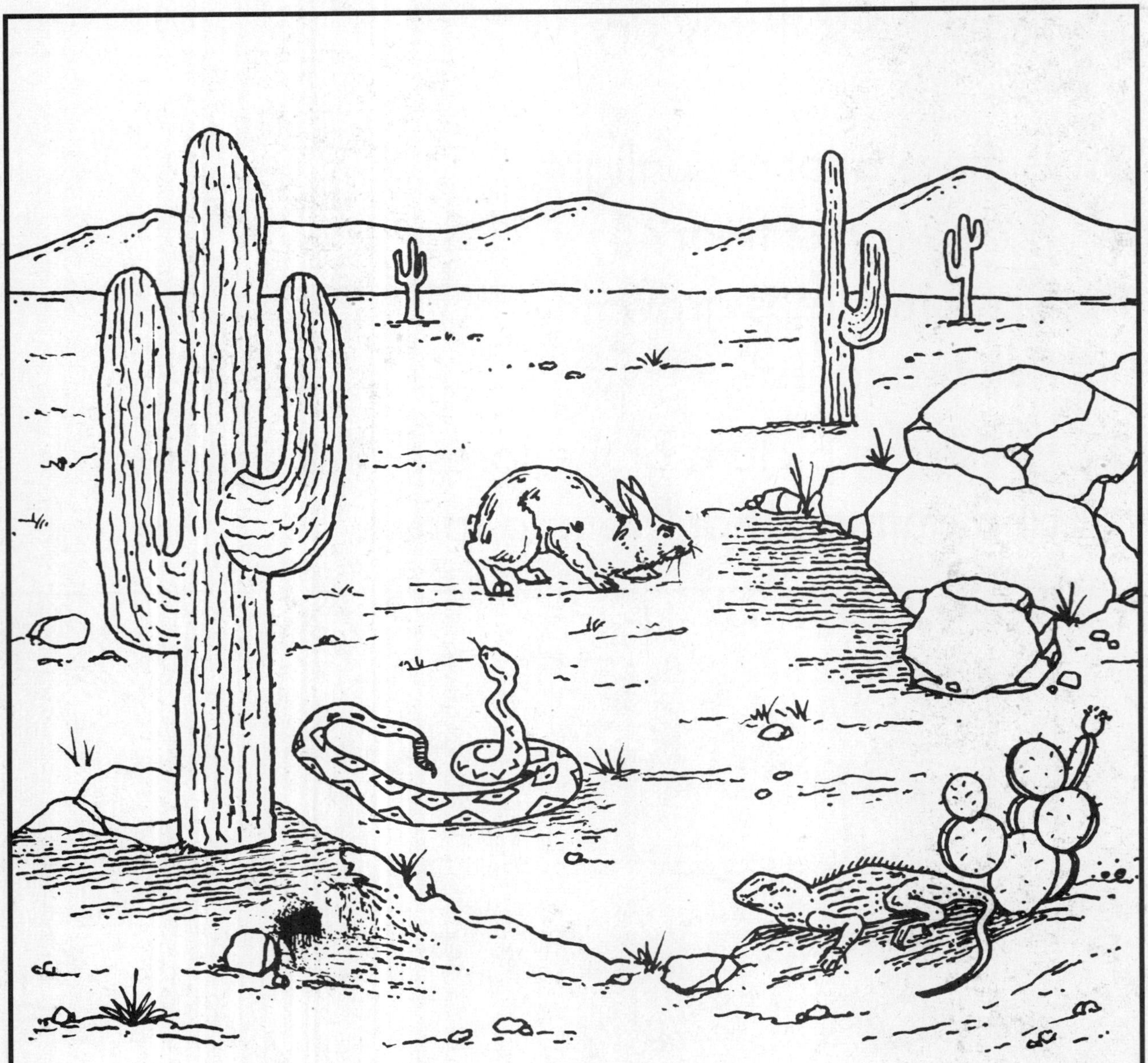

Name _____

 Concept Review

What Lives in the Desert?

1. Mark an **X** on the plants and animals that do not belong in the desert.

2. Circle the words that tell about a desert.

dry   wet   rainy

sunny   cactus   oak tree

Use with page B33.

Name _____

Communicate

1. Tell about plants that grow where there is little light. Write or draw.

_____
_____
_____
_____
_____
_____
_____

2. Tell about plants that grow where there is a lot of light. Write or draw.

_____
_____
_____
_____
_____
_____
_____

Name _____

What Lives in a Rain Forest?

1. Draw animals that live at each level of the rain forest.

Draw a line under the best answer.

2. Most rain forests are _____.

cool and dry   wet and warm   wet and cool

3. Plants that need a lot of light live at the _____ of the rain forest.

bottom   middle   top

Use with page B37.   Workbook • WB51

Name _____

Classify

Color the animals that live in the ocean.
Mark **X** through the animals that do **not**
live in the ocean.

1.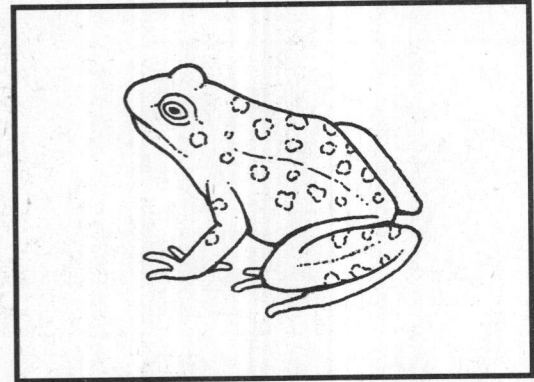

2.

3.

4.

5.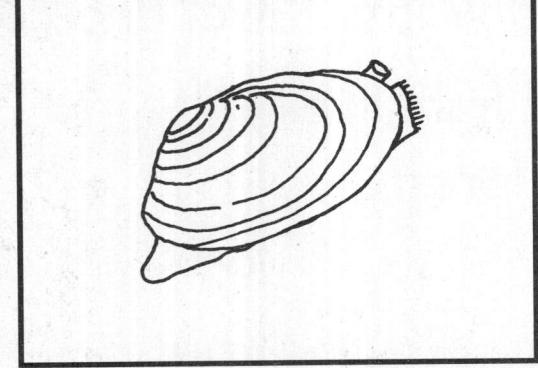

6.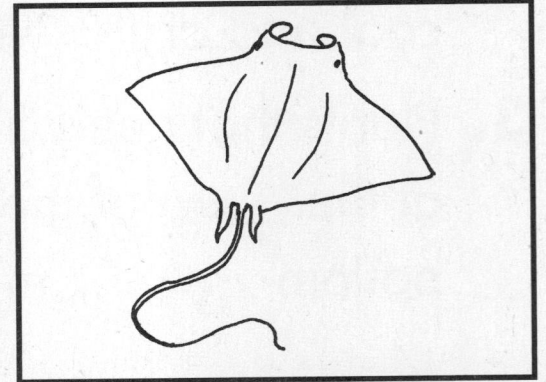

WB52 • Workbook

Use with page B38.

Name _____

What Lives in the Ocean?

1. Complete the picture. Show what helps the animal swim fast to catch food.

2. Circle the body parts that help the animals swim and steer.

3. Add algae to the picture. Draw the algae where it lives.

Name _____

A Place to Live

Label each picture. Use the words in the box.

| algae   desert   forest   ocean   rain forest |

1. _____

2. _____

3. _____

4. _____

5. _____

WB54 • Workbook

Use with pages B26–B41.

Name _____

Reading Skills Practice

Relate Pictures to Text

Rain forests are wet and warm. Plants and animals live at different levels of the rain forest. The rain forest gives plants and animals what they need to live.

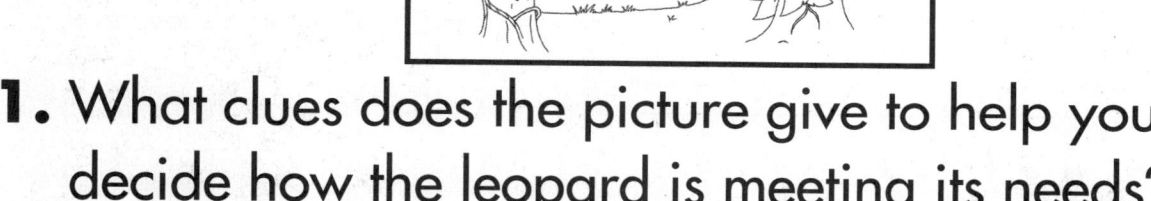

1. What clues does the picture give to help you decide how the leopard is meeting its needs?
_____
_____
_____
_____

2. What clues does the picture give to help you decide how the orchid is meeting its needs?
_____
_____
_____
_____

Use with page B40.   Workbook • WB55

Name _____

Write to Describe

A. Draw a plant or an animal that lives at each level of the rain forest.

In the treetops

In the middle of the branches

On the ground

B. Write describing words next to each picture you drew.

WB56 • Workbook

Use with pages B44–B45.

Name _____

Unit C, Chapter 1 Earth's Land

LESSON 1 What Can We Observe About Rocks?	LESSON 2 What Are Fossils?	LESSON 3 What Have We Learned from Fossils?
1. There are many different kinds of _____.	1. Plants and animals _____ lived on Earth _____ ago.	1. An _____ plant or animal is no longer living.
2. People use _____ in different ways.	2. _____ are the parts or imprints of plants or animals that lived long ago.	2. Some plants and animals today have _____ from long ago.

Use with page C3.

Workbook • WB57

Name _____

Classify

1. Classify the rocks. Color the large rocks **yellow**. Color the small rocks **blue**.

2. Classify the rocks another way. Color the smooth rocks **red**. Color the rough rocks **green**.

Name _____

What Can We Observe About Rocks?

1. Color the rocks **red**. Color the sand **yellow**.

2. People use rocks in different ways. Draw a picture that shows one way people use rocks.

Name _____

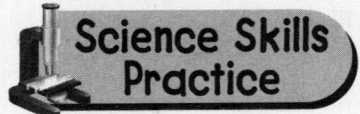

Make a Model

1. This leaf could become a fossil. Draw what the fossil might look like.

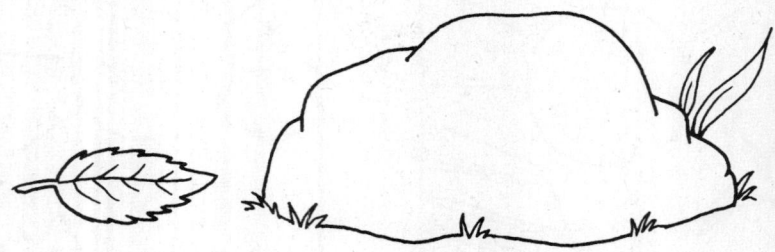

2. Make a drawing of some other thing that could become a fossil.

WB60 • **Workbook**   Use with page C8.

Name _____

What Are Some Kinds of Fossils?

Draw a line from the fossil to the living thing that made the fossil.

1.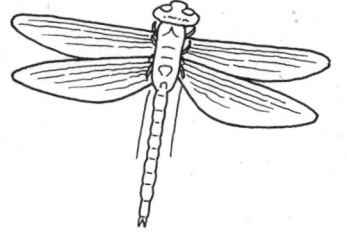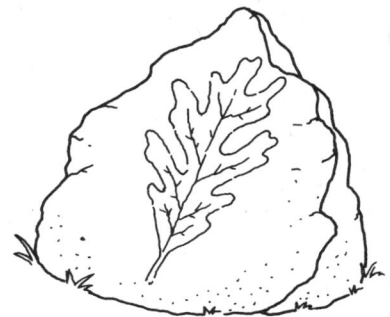

2.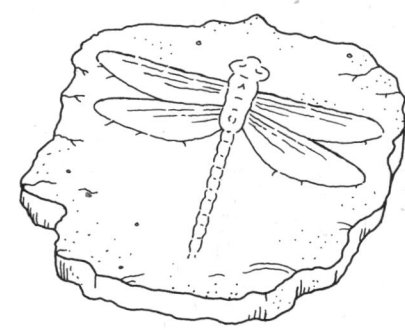

3.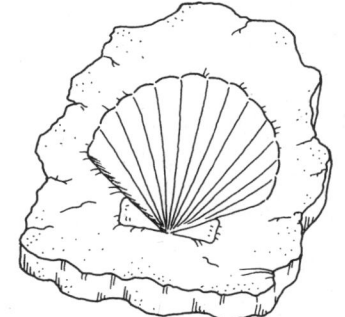

Use with page C11.   Workbook • WB61

Name _____

Compare

Describe each kind of fossil. Use the words in the box.

extinct animal   sea animal   plant

1. snail

_____
_____
_____

2. trilobite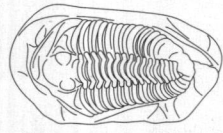

_____
_____
_____

3. fern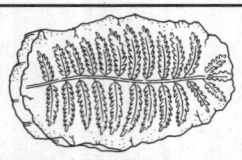

_____
_____
_____

WB62 • Workbook   Use with page C12.

Name _____

How Do Different Fossils Compare?

1. Color the plant fossils green. Color the animal fossils red.

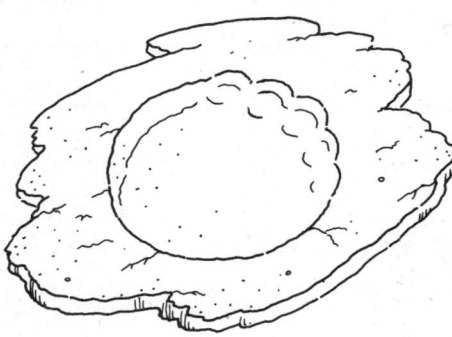

2. Circle the fossil of the animal that is extinct.

3. Mark an X over the fossil that shows the largest animal.

Use with page C15.

Name _____

Vocabulary Review

Earth's Land

Write a word from the box to fill in each blank.

| rock   fossils   extinct   sand |

1. Tiny pieces of rock are called _____.

2. Kinds of plants or animals that are no longer living are _____.

3. The parts and imprints of a plant or animal that lived long ago are called _____.

4. Fossils are usually found in _____.

Label the picture.

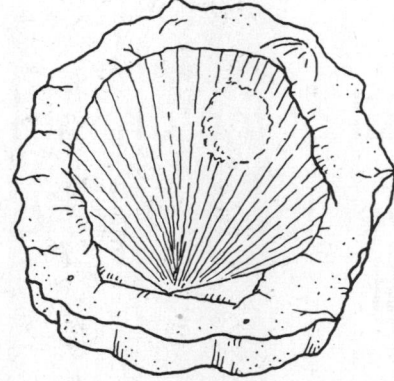

WB64 • Workbook

Use with pages C4–C15.

Name _____

Use Graphic Sources for Information

Kinds of Fossils There are many different types of fossils. Some are from animals, and others are from plants. Look at the pictures below. Tell whether each fossil is from a plant or an animal.

_____
_____

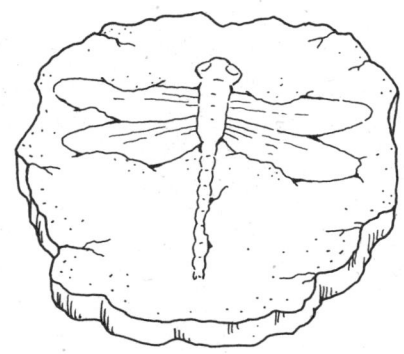

_____
_____

Use with page C10.

Tell a Story

A. Draw a picture of a starfish in a rock.

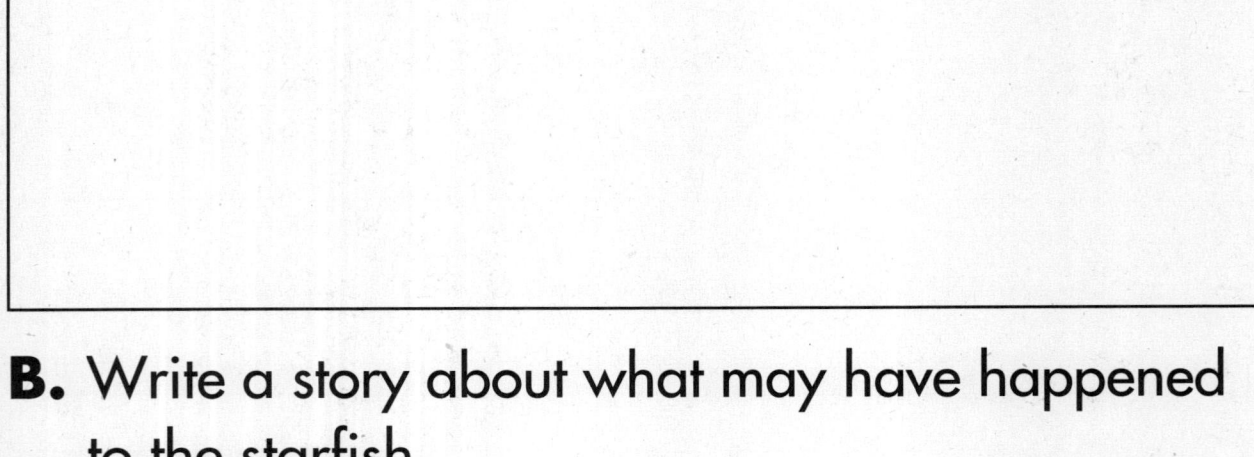

B. Write a story about what may have happened to the starfish.

_____
_____
_____
_____
_____

Name _____

Unit C, Chapter 2 Our Natural Resources

LESSON 1
What Are Natural Resources?

1. Something found in nature that people use is a _____ _____.

2. A _____ is a nonliving thing found in nature.

LESSON 2
Where Is Air on Earth?

1. You can _____ air but you can't see, smell, or _____ it.

2. Plants and animals need _____ to live.

LESSON 3
Where Is Fresh Water Found?

1. Fresh water is found in most streams, _____, and _____.

2. People need _____, fresh water.

LESSON 4
How Can People Take Care of Resources?

Three things people can do to take care of resources are: _____, _____, and _____.

Use with page C2.

Workbook • WB67

Name _____

Gather and Record Data

Look at the natural resources found here. How are they used? Record your data in the chart.

Natural Resource	How It Is Used
soil	
water	
apple tree	

WB68 • Workbook   Use with page C22.

Name _____

What Are Natural Resources?

Match the pictures to tell how people use natural resources.

1.

2.

3.

4. Draw how people use soil to get food. Color the soil brown.

Use with page C27.

Workbook • WB69

Name _____

Infer

Air is all around. You can not see air. But you can see what it does.

1. Circle in the picture the things that air is moving.
2. Put an **X** on something filled with air.
3. Color all the living things. They use air, too.

WB70 • Workbook Use with page C28.

Name _____

Where Is Air on Earth?

Color where the air is in each picture.

1.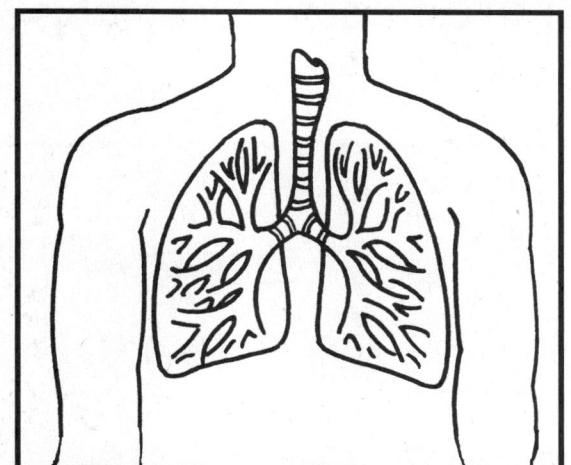

2.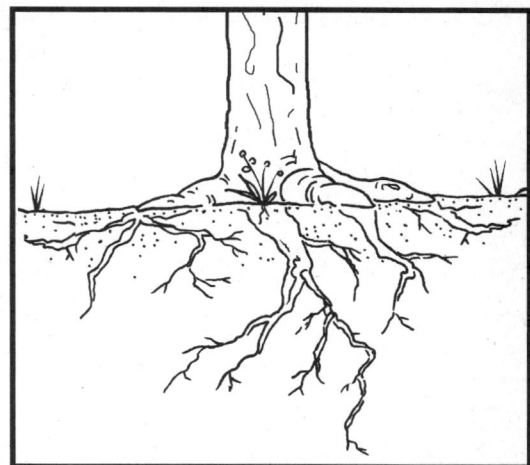

3.

4.

Answer **yes** or **no**.

5. You can see air. _____

6. You can feel air. _____

Use with page C31.   Workbook • WB71

Name _____

Draw a Conclusion

Rain and melted snow run down mountains. Snow and rain are fresh water.

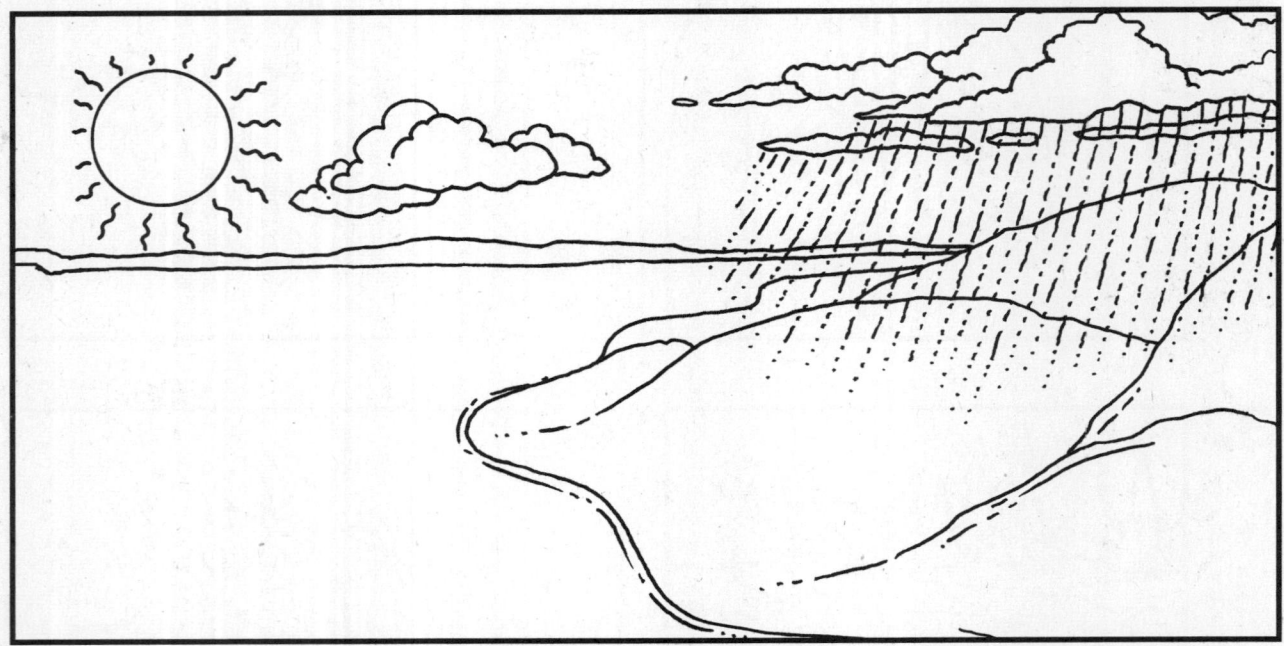

1. Color the fresh water **blue**.
2. Color the mountains **brown**.
3. Tell how you use fresh water.

_____
_____
_____
_____

Name _____

 Concept Review

Where Is Fresh Water Found?

Match to tell how people use fresh water.

1.

2.

- cooking

- washing

- drinking

3.

4. Draw a freshwater lake. Color it **blue**.

Use with page C35.

Name _____

Communicate

1. Write a sentence. Tell how this milk carton is being reused.

_____
_____
_____
_____

2. Susie is making a drawing with paper and crayons. Write a sentence. Tell how Susie can use less paper.

_____
_____
_____
_____

Name _____

How Can People Take Care of Resources?

1. Water is a natural resource. Which picture shows how to use <u>less</u> water? Mark an **X** over the picture that shows how the girl can use less water.

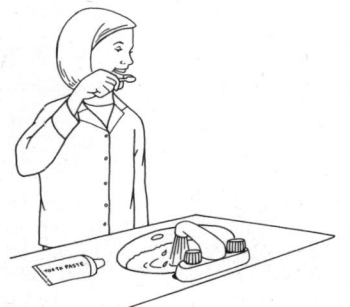 

Circle the best answer.

2. What helps natural resources last longer?

    recycling   throwing away

3. What is something you can recycle at home?

    newspaper   food

4. What happens if Earth's minerals are used up?

    more will grow   there will be no more

Use with page C41.

Name _____

Our Natural Resources

1. Color the fresh water blue. Color the air yellow. Circle the river.

Fill in the blank. Use the words in the box.

| reuse | reduce | natural resource | recycle |

2. A _____ is something found in nature that people can use.

3. When people use less of something, they _____ their use of them.

4. You can _____ something by using it again.

5. When you _____, you collect cans and newspapers to be made into new things.

WB76 • Workbook   Use with pages C22–C41.

Name _____

Recall Supporting Facts and Details

Fresh Water Fresh water is found in lakes, rivers, and streams. Rain is fresh water. People use fresh water for drinking, cooking, and washing.

Look at each picture. **X** the pictures that show fresh water.

Name _____

Write a Story

A. Draw a picture of recycling at your school.

B. Write a story about your picture. Include details about what you observe.

_____
_____
_____
_____
_____
_____
_____
_____

Name _____

Unit D, Chapter 2 The Sky and the Seasons

LESSON 1 What Can We See in the Sky?

1. You can see the _____, stars, and _____ in the sky.
2. The sun is a _____.

LESSON 2 Why Do We Have Day and Night?

1. The sun warms our land, _____, and _____.
2. When Earth _____ we have day and night.

LESSON 3 What Is Spring?

1. A season is a time of the _____.
2. Spring has warmer _____ than winter.

LESSON 4 What Is Summer?

1. Summer has the _____ hours of daylight.
2. The air is _____ in summer than in spring.

LESSON 5 What Is Fall?

1. Fall has _____ air than summer.
2. Plants stop _____.
3. Animals have less _____.

LESSON 6 What Is Winter?

1. Winter has fewer _____ of daylight than fall.
2. Some animals eat _____ food.

Use with page D25.

Name _____

Science Skills Practice

Communicate

1. Finish the chart. Look at the day sky and the night sky. Record what you see.

Things in the Day Sky	Things in the Night Sky

2. Write a sentence that tells about the night sky.

_____
_____
_____
_____

WB92 • Workbook   Use with page D26.

Name _____

What Can We See in the Sky?

1. Circle the things that are found in the night sky.

Circle the words that best finish the sentence.

2. Stars are objects in the sky that _____.

    are very close   give off light   you see in daylight

3. Mars, Venus, and Earth are all _____.

    stars   moons   planets

Use with page D29.

Name _____

Science Skills Practice

Make a Model

1. Draw an arrow from the sun to Earth.

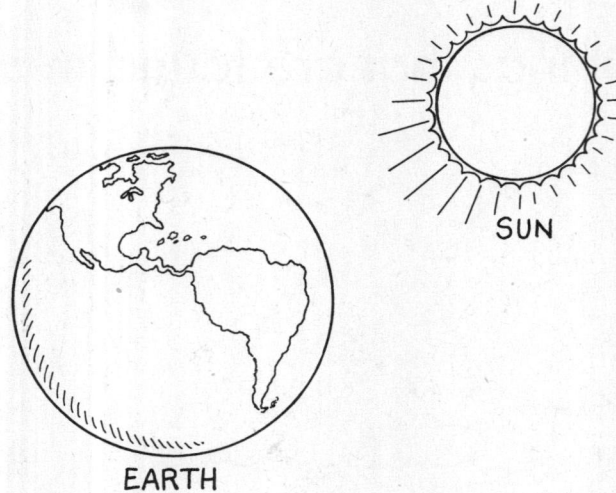

2. Mark an **X** on the part of Earth the sun shines on.

3. Look at the **X**. Is it day or night there?
_____
_____

4. Draw what the sky looks like during the day.

WB94 • Workbook   Use with page D30.

Name _____

Why Do We Have Day and Night?

1. Sometimes it is day, and sometimes it is night. Look at the X marked on Earth. Circle the picture that shows it is night where the X is.

Circle the words that best finish the sentence.

2. The sun gives off _____.

    daylight and   stars and   heat and
    darkness   moons   light

3. Earth is always moving because it _____.

    rotates   moves   shakes

Use with page D33.

Name _____

Science Skills Practice

Infer

1. Juan would like to grow beans. Color the picture that shows the best time to plant the seeds.

2. Tell why you colored that picture.

_____
_____
_____
_____
_____
_____

3. Circle the words that tell about what a seed needs to begin to grow.

water   warmth   light   air

WB96 • Workbook   Use with page D34.

Name _____

What Is Spring?

1. Circle the things that are found in spring.

2. Circle the words that best finish the sentence.

Spring has ____.

cooler air   falling leaves   more hours of daylight

3. Draw how growing plants help young animals.

Name _____

Science Skills Practice

Order

1. Write the temperatures from coolest to hottest.

_____
_____
_____
_____
_____
_____
_____
_____

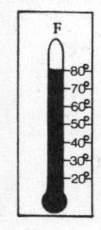 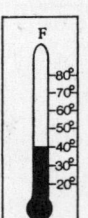

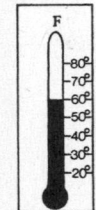 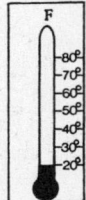

2. These words tell how a plant will grow. Draw pictures to show how a plant will grow.

| seed | sprout | flower |

WB98 • Workbook   Use with page D38.

Name _____

What Is Summer?

Animals look different in spring and summer. Tell which season each picture shows.

1. _____   2. _____

3. _____   4. _____

5. Draw flowers and trees in summer.

Use with page D41.

Name _____

Science Skills Practice

Predict

1. Draw what these trees will look like when they have fruit ready for picking. Color the fruit on each tree.

orange tree   **cherry tree**

2. In spring, this kitten was born. In summer, it grew. Draw what the kitten will look like next.

Name _____

What Is Fall?

Circle the answer that fits the sentence best.

1. The season that follows summer is ____ .

   spring   fall

2. In fall there are ____ hours of daylight.

   less   more

3. In some places, leaves change in fall. Draw one of those places. Color it.

   [ ]

4. It is fall. Tell what this animal is doing.

   _____
   _____
   _____

Use with page D45.

Name _____

Investigate

1. Circle the gloves that are best for keeping warm.

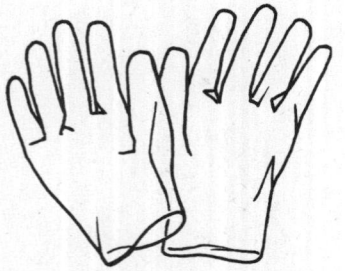 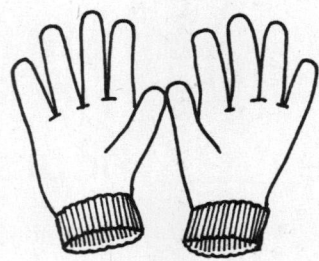 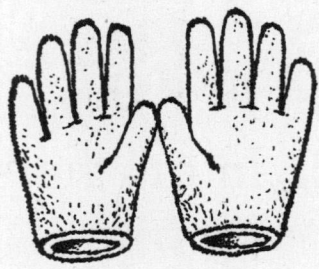

2. Carol has a pair of boots. One boot has a hole. Tell how Carol could investigate which boot has a hole. Draw pictures of the things she could use to help.

_____
_____
_____
_____
_____
_____

Name _____

What Is Winter?

1. Color the winter tree **blue**. Color the spring tree **green**. Color the summer tree **yellow**. Color the fall tree **red**. Label the season for each picture.

_____

_____

_____

_____

2. Tell what a plant might look like in winter.

_____

_____

Use with page D49.   Workbook • **WB103**

Name _____

The Sky and the Seasons

Label each picture. Use the words in the box.

| spring   sun   summer   fall   moon   winter |

1. _____

2. _____

3. _____

4. _____

These sentences are **false**. Change the underlined words to make the sentences **true**.

5. We have day and night because Earth <u>stops</u>. _____

6. The <u>sun</u> is the brightest object in the sky at night. _____

WB104 • Workbook   Use with pages D26–D49.

Name _____

Identify Cause and Effect

Plants and Animals in Summer Read the sentences. Draw an arrow from the cause to the effect.

Cause	Effect
1. Lots of sunlight helps plants grow.	They begin to look like adult birds.
2. Young birds lose their first feathers.	They become strong and fast.
3. Young foals eat and grow.	Flowers begin to form.

Wearing white can help keep you cool on a hot day. Write how this boy might feel.

_____
_____

Use with page D36.

Name _____

Write to Describe

Draw your neighborhood as it looks in each season. Write a sentence to describe each picture.

Spring	Summer

_____
_____
_____
_____

Fall	Winter

_____
_____
_____
_____

WB106 • Workbook   Use with pages D52–D53.

Name _____

Unit E, Chapter 1 Investigate Matter

LESSON 1 What Can We Observe About Solids?

1. Everything around us is _____.

2. Solids are matter that keep their _____.

3. Solids can be sorted in many _____.

LESSON 2 What Can We Observe About Liquids?

1. Matter that flows is called a _____.

2. Liquids take the _____ of what they are poured into.

3. Some liquids mix with water, but _____ does not.

LESSON 3 What Objects Sink or Float?

1. Some objects float and some objects _____.

2. Changing the _____ of an object helps it sink or float.

LESSON 4 What Solids Dissolve in Liquids?

1. Some solids _____ in liquids.

2. Soil and _____ do not dissolve in water.

LESSON 5 What Can We Observe About Gases?

1. Gas spreads out and takes the _____ of its container.

2. You can not see _____ but you can see what they do.

LESSON 6 How Can We Change Objects?

1. You can change objects by _____ or bending them.

2. You can change objects by _____ or mixing them.

Use with page E3.

Workbook • WB107

Name _____

Classify

1. Group the objects that are the same. Draw your groups in the chart.

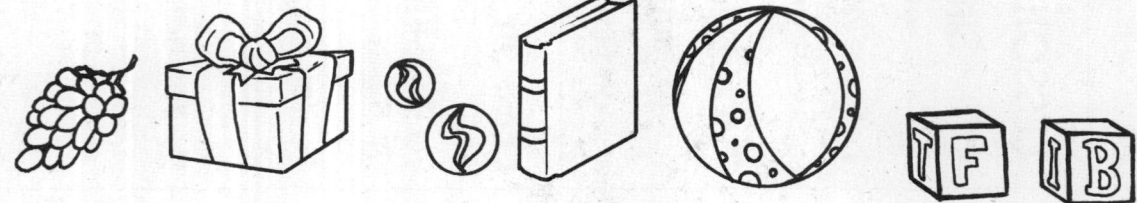

My Groups	
Group 1	**Group 2**

2. Tell why you grouped the objects as you did.

_____

_____

_____

WB108 • Workbook

Use with page E4.

Name _____

What Can We Observe About Solids?

1. Draw something that is matter.

2. Color the solids **red**.

3. How is this man changing a solid?
_____
_____
_____

Use with page E7.

Name _____

Use Numbers

1. Circle the container you think has more water.

   A   **B**

2. Circle the tool you could use to measure the water.

    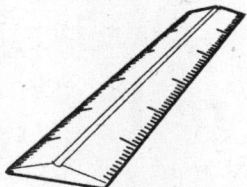 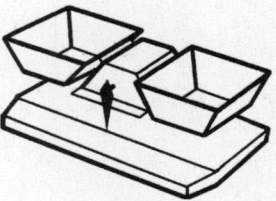

3. Jill measured the water in each container. Both containers had 12 ounces. Circle the words that tell about the containers.

   Container A ____.

   a. has more water than Container B

   b. has the same amount of water as Container B

   c. has less water than Container B

4. Why does B look as if it has more water than A?
   _____
   _____

WB110 • Workbook   Use with page E8.

Name _____

 Concept Review

What Can We Observe About Liquids?

1. Draw liquids in the containers.

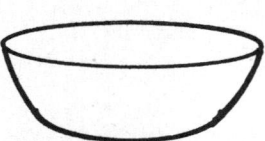  

2. Circle the liquid that does not mix with water.

3. Circle the things that are liquid.

 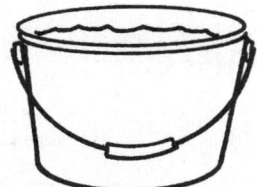 

Use with page E11.   Workbook • WB111

Name _____

Gather and Record Data

1. Observe the picture. Record in the chart the liquids and solids.

Matter	
Liquids	**Solids**

2. How many solids are there? _____

3. How many liquids are there? _____

WB112 • Workbook   Use with page E12.

Name _____

What Objects Sink or Float?

Circle **float** or **sink** for each picture.

1.

   float   sink

2.

   float   sink

3.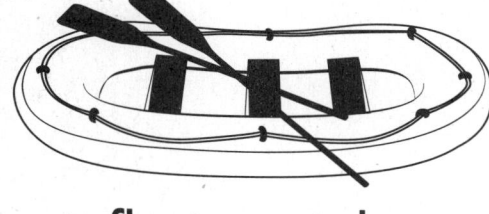

   float   sink

4.

   float   sink

5. Draw something that floats and something that sinks. Color the object that floats **red**. Color the object that sinks **blue**.

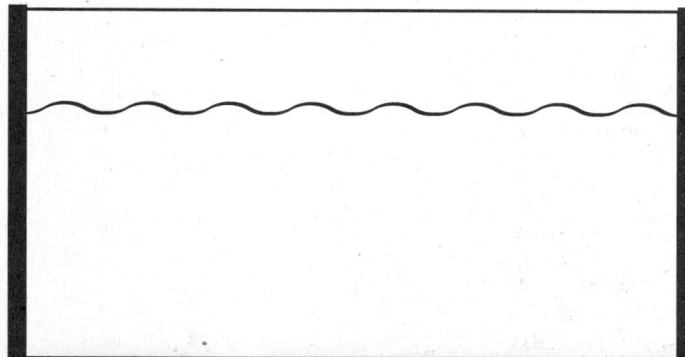

Use with page E15.

Name _____

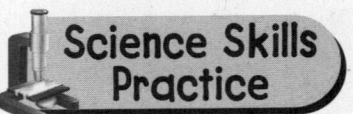

Form a Hypothesis

Use terms from the box to help you form a hypothesis. Write it.

1. A tea bag is placed in a cup of hot water.

| water | dissolve | tea |

_____
_____

2. A rock is dropped into a container of water.

| rock | water | sink |

_____
_____

3. A chef stirs a cup filled with vinegar and water.

| mix | water | vinegar |

_____
_____

WB114 • Workbook   Use with page E16.

Name _____

 Concept Review

What Solids Dissolve in Liquids?

1. Circle the solids that dissolve in water.

2. Circle the solids that do not dissolve in water.

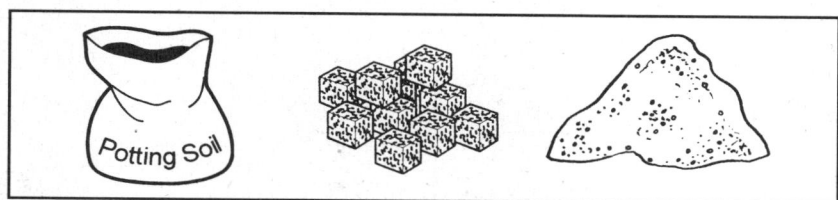

3. In what temperature of a liquid will solids dissolve faster?

    hot   cold

4. Complete the sentence below.
A solid dissolves in a liquid when

_____

_____

_____ .

Name _____

Draw a Conclusion

1. These spoons had different liquids on them. Why is one liquid still on the spoon?

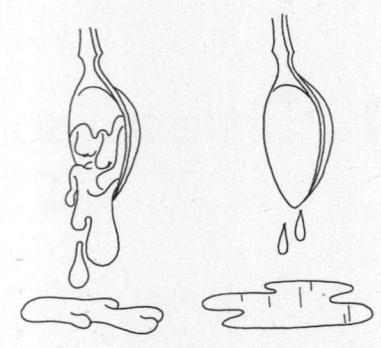

_____
_____
_____
_____

2. The boy has the same balloon in both pictures. Why does the balloon look different in the second picture?

_____
_____
_____
_____

3. What happened to the clay?

_____
_____
_____

Name _____

What Can We Observe About Gases?

1. There is gas in each container. Color the space the gas takes up.

  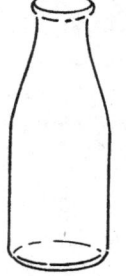

2. Color where the gas is in this liquid.

3. You can not see air. How do you know it is here?

_____
_____

Use with page E23.   Workbook • WB117

Name _____

Investigate

1. These pictures are not finished. Finish each picture a different way.

2. These pictures are the same. Color each picture to make it look different.

WB118 • Workbook Use with page E24.

Name _____

 Concept Review

How Can We Change Objects?

1. This toy is made of wire. Draw how you could bend it to make it look different.

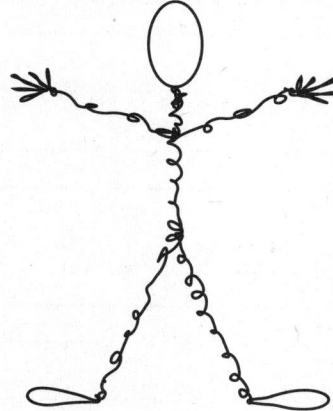

2. You could change this paper with scissors. Draw how it would look after you cut it.

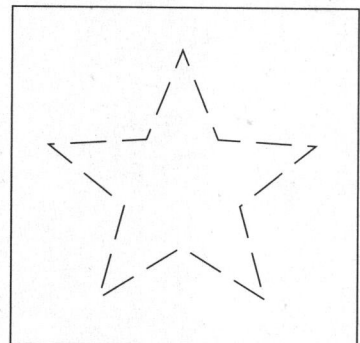

3. Finish the sentence. Circle the best word.

_____ changes liquid juice to a frozen ice pop.

Melting   Freezing   Mixing

Use with page E27.   Workbook • WB119

Name _____

Matter

Write your answer. Use the words in the box.

| gas | liquid | matter |

1. I am all around you. What am I? _____
2. I take up the shape of my container. What am I? _____
3. I can flow fast or slow. What am I? _____

Match the word to the picture that tells about it.

4. solids •   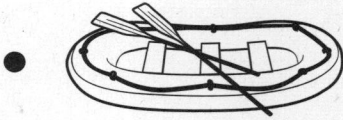 •

5. sink •    •

6. float •    •

7. change •    •

8. dissolve •   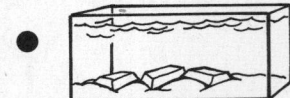 •

Name _____

Use Graphic Sources for Information

How Objects React on Water

Use the chart to answer the questions.

Objects That Sink	Objects That Float
marble	beach ball
rock	driftwood
anchor	toy boat
	plastic cup

1. How many objects float? ____ How many sink? ____

2. Circle the object that you might find at the bottom of a pond.

3. Which objects would be best used in a fish tank? Circle your answers.

Use with page E10.

Name _____

Write to Compare and Contrast

A. Draw a container of a thin liquid and a container of a thick liquid that you like to drink. Label your pictures.

| **Thin Liquid:** _____ | **Thick Liquid:** _____ |

B. Write about how these liquids are alike.

_____
_____
_____

C. Write about how these liquids are different.

_____
_____
_____

WB122 • Workbook   Use with pages E30–E31.

Name _____

Unit E, Chapter 2 Making Sound

LESSON 1 What Are Sounds?	LESSON 2 How Are Sounds Different?	LESSON 3 What Sounds Do Instruments Make?
1. Sound is made when objects _____. 2. You hear _____ all around you.	1. Sounds are _____. 2. Sounds can be quiet or _____. 3. The _____ of a sound is how high or low the sound is.	1. Musical instruments make _____ when a part vibrates. 2. Each instrument has its own _____.

Use with Page E33.

Workbook • WB123

Name _____

Investigate

1. This guitar makes sound. Color the part that vibrates to make sound.

Match the sound to the thing that makes it.

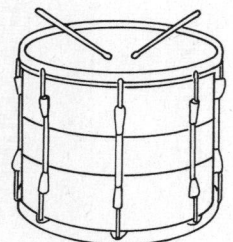

2. ring

3. boom

4. shhh

WB124 • Workbook

Use with page E34.

Name _____

What Are Sounds?

1. Mark an X on all the things that are making sounds.

Circle the word that best finishes each sentence.

2. Sound is made when things _____.

    stand still   vibrate

3. When strings on a violin stop vibrating, the sound _____.

    stops   gets louder

Use with page E37.   Workbook • WB125

Name _____

Use Numbers

Each bottle has a different pitch.

high pitch

low pitch

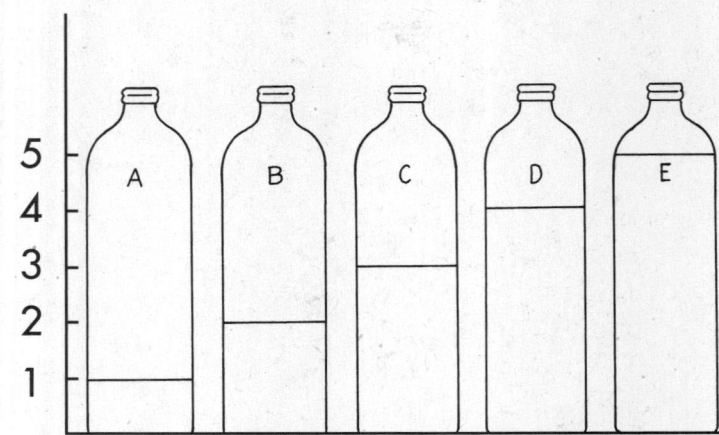

Circle the best answer to each question.

1. Which bottle has the highest pitch when you blow across its top?

   Bottle A   Bottle C   Bottle E

2. Which bottle has the lowest pitch when you blow across its top?

   Bottle A   Bottle C   Bottle E

Name _____

How Are Sounds Different?

1. Circle the things that make loud sounds. Mark an **X** over the things that make soft sounds.

2. Write the word that best finishes the sentence.

| loud | low |

_____

The pitch is how high or _____ the sound is.

Name _____

Science Skills Practice

Form a Hypothesis

1. What kinds of sounds do these instruments make? Draw a line to the word in the box that tells your answer.

 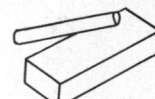 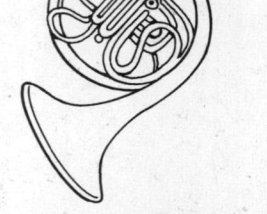

| tap | honk | ding |

2. What part of this instrument is missing? Draw what is missing.

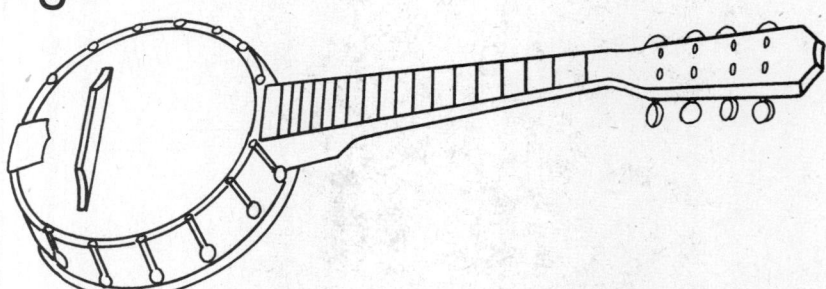

3. Write a sentence about how you can make the banjo make noise.

_____
_____
_____
_____

WB128 • Workbook   Use with page E46.

Name _____

What Sounds Do Instruments Make?

1. Color the part of the instrument that vibrates to make sound.

These children are making music.

Write a sentence that tells how the musical instruments are different.

_____
_____
_____
_____

Use with page E49.

Name _____

Vocabulary Review

Making Sound

These sentences are false. Change the underlined word to make the sentence true.

1. To move back and forth very fast is to <u>hum</u>. _____

2. <u>Music</u> is how high or low a sound is. _____

Circle the word that best finishes the sentence.

3. Everything you hear is _____.

   loud   sound   soft

4. A _____ is something used to make music.

   musical instrument   loud   pitch

Look at the picture.
X the part that vibrates.

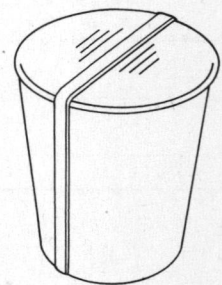

WB130 • Workbook   Use with pages E33–E53.

Name _____

Recall Supporting Facts and Details

Read the story below. Then answer the questions.

Max likes to make his guitar sound right. Before he plays it, he always tunes it. To do this, he has to turn the keys. Turning the keys one way makes the strings get tighter. The sound goes higher. Turning the keys the other way makes the sound go lower. The strings get looser. Max can make his guitar sound right by changing the way the strings sound.

What is the main idea?
_____
_____
_____

Draw a line under some ways Max makes his guitar sound good.

Use with page E42.

Name _____

Write to Describe

A. Make up a musical instrument. Draw a picture of your instrument. Give your instrument a name.

My musical instrument is called a
_____
_____.

B. Write about your musical instrument. Describe how it sounds. Describe its pitch.

_____
_____
_____
_____
_____
_____

WB132 • Workbook   Use with pages E52–E53.

Name _____

Unit F, Chapter 1 Pushes and Pulls

LESSON 1
What Makes Things Move?

1. A _____ is a push or a pull.

2. When you _____ something, you press it away.

LESSON 2 What Are Some Ways Things Move?

1. Things move in many _____ ways.

2. One way to tell how a thing moves is by the _____ it makes.

LESSON 3 Why Do Things Move the Way They Do?

1. Motion changes when you _____ or _____ something.

2. A hard push will move something _____.

LESSON 4
How Do Objects Move on Surfaces?

1. Friction makes it _____ to move objects.

2. A _____ surface makes more friction than a smooth surface.

LESSON 5
How Do Wheels Help Objects Move?

1. A _____ is a roller that turns on an axle.

2. Wheels and rollers make things _____ to push and pull.

Use with page F3.   Workbook • WB133

Name _____

Investigate

These logs need to be moved from the pile to the campfire.

1. Circle the things that could help you move the logs.

2. Tell how you could move a pencil across a desk.

_____
_____
_____
_____

WB134 • Workbook   Use with page F4.

Name _____

What Makes Things Move?

Tell how each thing is being moved.
Write **push** or **pull**.

1. _____   **2.** _____   **3.** _____

4. Show what the ball will do when the girl kicks it. Draw an arrow.

Use with page F7.   Workbook • WB135

Name _____

Group

1. Circle the toys you push. Make an **X** on the toys you pull.

2. Mark an **X** on objects that move easily with a gentle push.

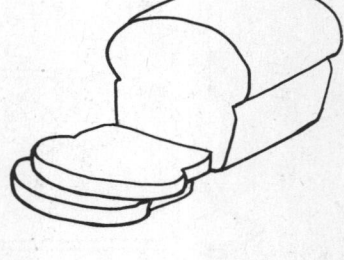

WB136 • Workbook

Use with page F8.

Name _____

What Are Some Ways Things Move?

Match the objects to the words that tell how each moves.

1. straight •   •

2. fast •   •

3. slow •   •

4. zigzag •   •

5. round and round •   •

6. back and forth •   •

Use with page F11.

Name _____

Predict

Kathy made a ramp. She put a marble at the top of her ramp.

1. What will happen when Kathy lets go of the marble? Draw a line to show where it will go.

2. This ramp is curved. Draw a line to show where Kathy's marble will go.

Name _____

Why Do Things Move the Way They Do?

1. Circle the push that will make a toy car go a short way.

hard push

gentle push

2. Show how the soccer ball might change direction on the playing field. Draw arrows.

3. What will happen when the balls bump together? Write or draw your ideas.

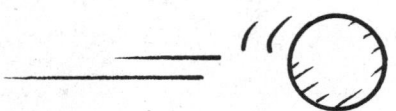 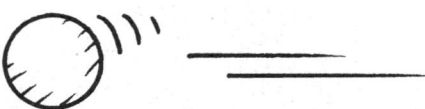

_____
_____

Use with page F17.

Workbook • WB139

Name _____

Measure

Marble 1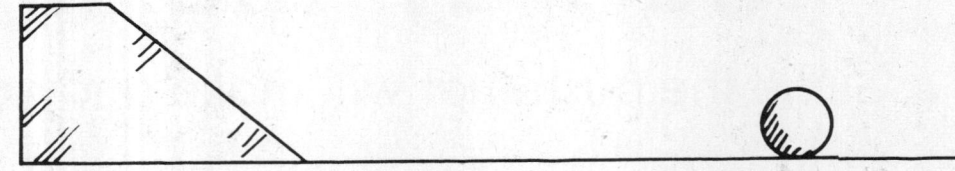

Marble 2

1. Measure how far each marble rolled. Write your answers.

_____   _____
           Marble 1   Marble 2

2. Circle the marble that rolled the farthest. Tell why.
_____
_____
_____
_____

WB140 • Workbook   Use with page F18.

Name _____

 Concept Review

How Do Surfaces Change the Way Objects Move?

Tell if each surface is **rough** or **smooth**. Circle your answer.

1.

rough   smooth

2.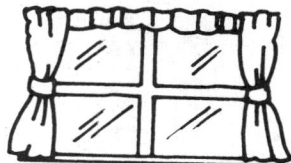

rough   smooth

3.

rough   smooth

4.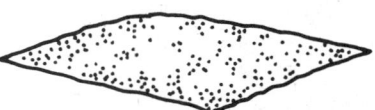

rough   smooth

5. Circle the road with more friction.

Use with page F21.   Workbook • WB141

Name _____

Science Skills Practice

Draw a Conclusion

Mike and Jenny rode on different paths.

Mike

Jenny

1. Circle the child that would be more tired after the ride. Tell why.
_____
_____
_____

2. Joyce made this toy. Draw something that you could add to make it easier to move.

WB142 • Workbook   Use with page F22.

Name _____

How Do Wheels Make Objects Easier to Move?

1. Draw wheels on the things that need wheels to move.

2. Circle the thing that will make the refrigerator move the easiest.

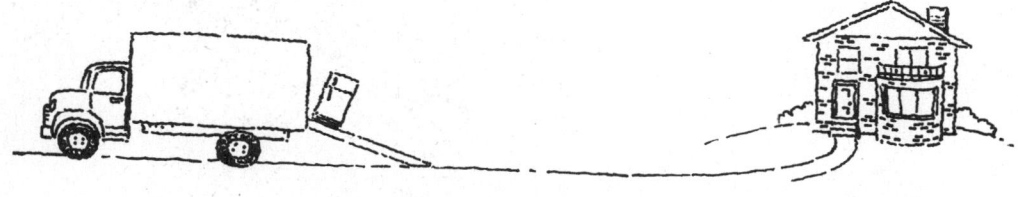

Use with page F25.

Name _____

Pushes and Pulls

Circle the word that best finishes each sentence.

1. When you ____ something, you tug it closer to you.

   A wheel   **B** push   **C** pull

2. A ____ is a push or a pull.

   A surface   **B** force   **C** zigzag

3. When you ____ something, you press it away from you.

   A push   **B** pull   **C** motion

4. When two surfaces rub together, it is called ____.

   A motion   **B** zigzag   **C** friction

5. Moving from one place to another is called ____.

   A motion   **B** friction   **C** surface

Name _____

Identify Cause and Effect

Why Things Move the Way They Do

Susan and her classmates were playing volleyball. When the ball came to Susan, she hit it over the net. The other team members hit it back over. One time, the ball hit the pole on the net and bounced out of bounds. Another time, someone hit the ball very hard. The ball bounced high off the ground. Finish the chart.

Cause	Effect
The ball came to Susan.	She hit the ball over the net.
	The ball bounced out of bounds.
Someone hit the ball very hard.	

Use with page F16.

Name _____

Write to Explain

A. Draw a picture of your favorite sport or game. Be sure to show pushes and pulls.

[ ]

B. Draw circles around the pushes in the picture. Draw squares around the pulls in the picture.

C. Write about how your favorite sport or game uses pushes and pulls.

_____
_____
_____
_____

WB146 • Workbook   Use with pages F28–F29.

Name _____

Unit F, Chapter 2 Magnets

LESSON 1
What Are Magnets?

1. Magnets are pieces of _____ that attract things.

2. Magnets can _____ things made of iron.

3. People use different kinds of _____ in different ways.

LESSON 2
What Are the Poles of a Magnet?

1. Poles are places on a magnet where the pull is the _____.

2. Every magnet has a _____ pole and a _____ pole.

3. Two poles that are the same _____ each other.

LESSON 3
What Can a Magnet Pull Through?

1. The pull of a magnet is called _____ force.

2. Magnetic force can pass through _____, water, air, _____, and _____.

LESSON 4
How Can You Make a Magnet?

1. A magnet can _____ an object made of iron.

2. You can make a magnet by _____ an iron object with a _____.

Use with page F31.

Workbook • WB147

Name _____

Record Data

Gather and circle the things that are pulled by a magnet. Make an **X** on the things that are **not** pulled by a magnet.

1.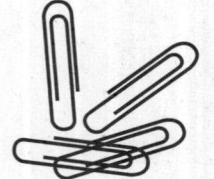
paper clips

2.
wax paper

3.
steel nail

4.
candle

5.
scissors

6.
yarn

7. Record your data in this chart.

My Chart	
Pulled by a magnet	**NOT pulled by a magnet**

Name _____

What Are Magnets?

Circle each object that a magnet would attract.

1.
leaf

2.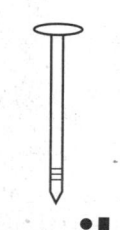
nail

3.
pencil

4.
thread

5.
key

6.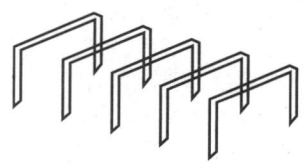
staples

Match each magnet to the words that tell what the magnet does.

7. picks things up •

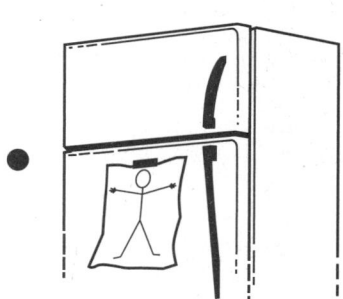

•

8. holds things together •

•

Use with page F37.

Workbook • WB149

Name _____

Infer

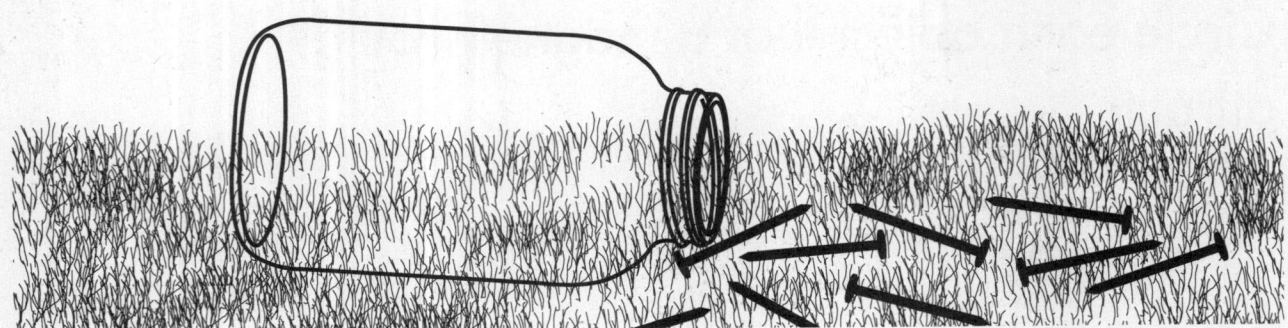

1. A man dropped a jar of nails in tall grass. What would you use to help him pick up the nails? Color the **best** answer.

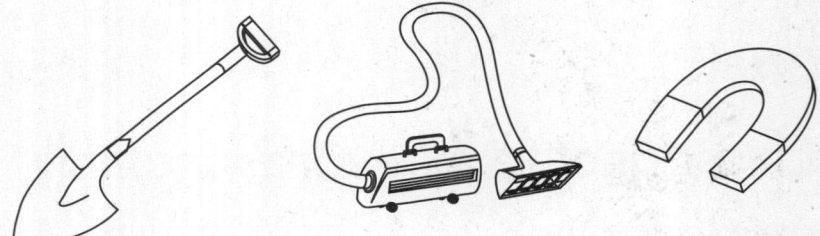

2. Tell why you would choose that item.
_____
_____
_____
_____

3. What kinds of things would a magnet pick up? Circle the **best** answer.

plastic   wood   iron

Name _____

What Are the Poles of a Magnet?

1. Match each word to the picture it tells about.

repel •

attract •

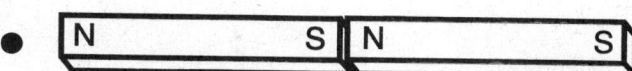

2. Write **S** and **N** to show how these magnets attract.

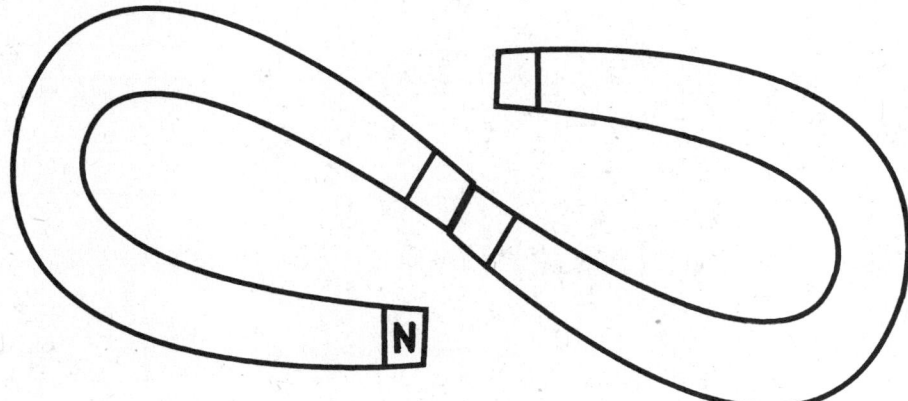

3. The magnet attracts iron bits. Color the parts of the magnet that have the strongest force.

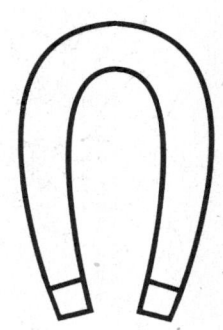

Use with page F41.

Workbook • WB151

Name _____

Plan an Investigation

How many paper clips can a magnet pick up?

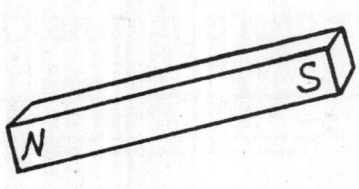
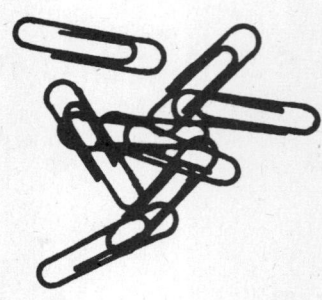

1. Tell how you could investigate this question.

_____
_____
_____
_____
_____
_____

2. Draw how your magnet looks as you investigate.

Name _____

What Can a Magnet Pull Through?

1. Joey wants to move a nail with a magnet. Circle the picture that will work the **best** for Joey.

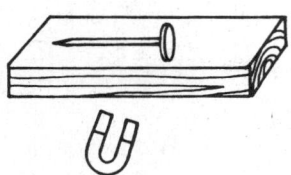 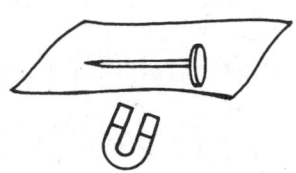 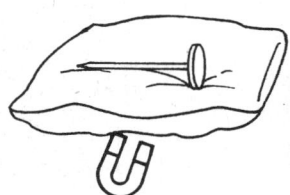

2. Circle all the things that the magnetic force of a small magnet can pass through.

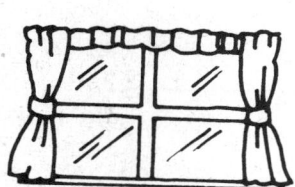  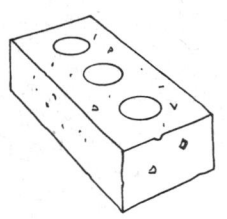 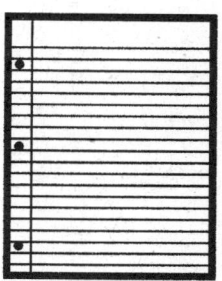

3. Circle the things that can be attracted with magnetic force.

   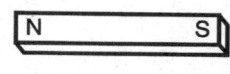

Use with page F45.   Workbook • WB153

Name _____

Draw a Conclusion

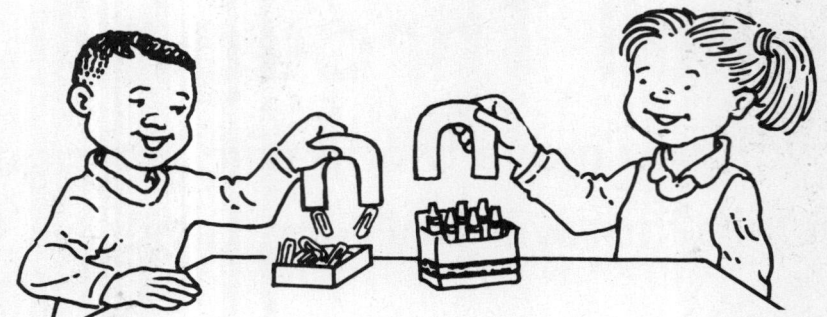

1. Edie and Harry are fishing with magnets. Edie's magnet does not lift the crayons. Tell why.

_____
_____

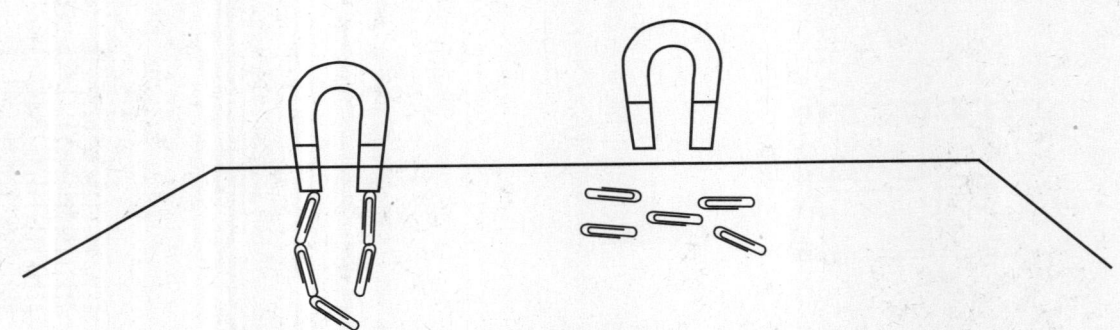

Magnet A   **Magnet B**

2. Magnet A lifted paper clips. Magnet B did not. Tell why.

_____
_____
_____

Name _____

How Can You Make a Magnet?

1. Color the objects that are magnetized.

   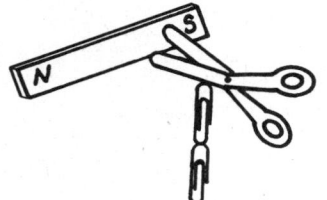   

2. Circle the object you would use to magnetize a nail.

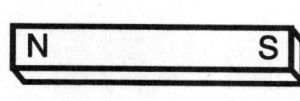      

3. How many paper clips have been magnetized?

one   two   five

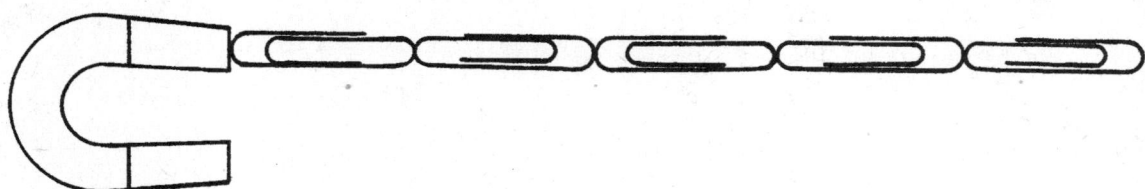

Use with page F49.   Workbook • WB155

Name _____

Magnets

Circle **true** or **false**. If the sentence is false, change the underlined word to make it true.

1. <u>Attract</u> means to pull something.
_____
_____   true   false

2. A <u>pole</u> is a piece of iron that attracts things.
_____
_____   true   false

3. How strongly a magnet pulls is its <u>strength</u>.
_____
_____   true   false

4. A magnet is <u>weakest</u> at its poles.
_____
_____   true   false

5. To repel means to <u>pull</u> something.
_____
_____   true   false

6. A magnet can <u>magnetize</u> a paper clip.
_____
_____   true   false

Name _____

Reading Skills Practice

Draw Conclusions

Magnets Magnets attract things made of iron. A magnet can magnetize, or give magnetic force to, the things it attracts. Mr. Smith ran a key over a magnet ten times the same way. Then he used the key to pick up some staples and paper clips.

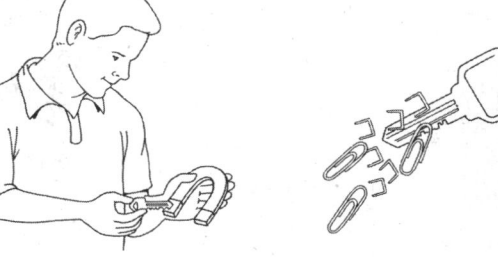

1. What did Mr. Smith do to his key?
_____
_____
_____
_____

2. Why did Mr. Smith's key pick up staples and paper clips?
_____
_____
_____
_____

Use with page F48.   Workbook • WB157

Name _____

 Writing Practice

Write Directions

A. Make up a game or a toy that uses magnets. Draw your game or toy in the box.

B. Write directions for playing your game or using your toy. Tell what to do first, next, and last.

First _____

Next _____

Last _____

WB158 • Workbook   Use with pages F52–F53.

Unit Experiments
Grade 1

Introduction to Unit Experiments **160**

UNIT A

Seeds and Water **163**

UNIT B

Animal Coverings **166**

UNIT C

Clean Air **169**

UNIT D

Heat and Water **172**

UNIT E

Solids and Water **175**

UNIT F

Height and Distance **178**

Name _____ **Experiment Log**

1. Observe and ask a question.

_____
_____
_____
_____
_____
_____

2. Form a hypothesis.
A hypothesis is a suggested answer to the question you are investigating. You must be able to do a fair test of the hypothesis.

_____
_____
_____
_____

3. Plan a fair test.
What things will you keep the same in the test? Write or draw them here.

Name _____   **Experiment Log**

4. What is one thing you will change in the test?

_____
_____
_____
_____

5. What objects will you need to do the test? List or draw them here.

6. What steps will you take to do the test? List or draw them here.

Name _____

Experiment Log

7. Do the test.
Record your data in a chart.

8. Draw conclusions. Communicate results.
What are your results? How can you communicate your results to others?

_____
_____
_____
_____
_____

Name _____

Unit A Experiment Log

Seeds and Water

Observe and ask a question.

1. What question can you ask about what seeds need to sprout?

_____
_____

Form a hypothesis.

2. What is something you think is true about what seeds need to sprout?

_____
_____

Plan a fair test.

3. What things will you keep the same in your test? Write or draw them here.

Use with page A1.

Name _____ Experiment Log

4. What one thing will you change in your test?

5. What things will you need to do your test? Write or draw them here.

6. What steps will you take to do your test?

Name _____   **Experiment Log**

Do the test.

7. Record your data in the chart.

Did Seeds Sprout Roots?

	Moist Seeds	**Dry Seeds**
Day 1		
Day 2		
Day 3		
Day 4		
Day 5		
Day 6		
Day 7		

Draw conclusions. Communicate results.

8. What are your results? How can you communicate your results to others?

_____
_____
_____
_____
_____
_____

Use with page A1.

Name _____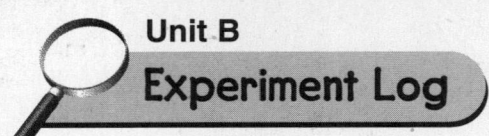

Animal Coverings

Observe and ask a question.

1. What can you ask about how body coverings help animals?
_____
_____
_____

Form a hypothesis.

2. What is something you think is true about how body coverings help animals?
_____
_____
_____

Plan a fair test.

3. What things will you keep the same in the test? Write or draw them here.

Name _____

4. What one thing will you change in the test?

5. What objects will you need to do the test? Write or draw them here.

6. What steps will you take to do the test?

Name _____

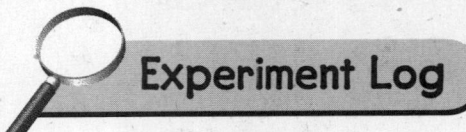

Do the test.

7. Record your data in the chart.

How Did the Covered Hand Feel?

Body Covering	Observation

Draw conclusions. Communicate results.

8. What are your results? How can you communicate your results to others?

_____
_____
_____
_____

Name _____

**Unit C
Experiment Log**

Clean Air

Observe and ask a question.

1. Air is dirty in some places. It is clean in other places. Ask a question about air in different places.

_____
_____
_____

Form a hypothesis.

2. Where do you think air is the cleanest?

_____
_____
_____

Plan a fair test.

3. What things will you keep the same in the test? Write or draw them here.

Use with page C1.   (page 1 of 3)   Workbook • WB169

Name _____ Experiment Log

4. What one thing will you change in the test?

5. What things will you need to do the test? Write or draw them here.

6. What steps will you take to do the test?

Name _____

Experiment Log

Do the test.

7. Record your data in the chart.

Where Is Air the Dirtiest?

Plate Number	Where It Was	Things I See

Draw conclusions. Communicate results.

8. What are your results? How can you communicate your results to others?

_____
_____
_____
_____
_____
_____

Name _____

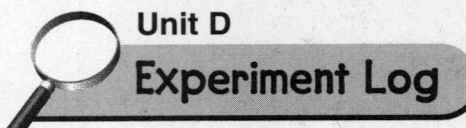

Heat and Water

Observe and ask a question.

1. The sun gives off heat. Can the sun's heat change water? Ask a question about the way heat can change water.

_____
_____

Form a hypothesis.

2. How do you think heat changes water?

_____
_____

Plan a fair test.

3. What things will you keep the same in your test? Write or draw them here.

Name _____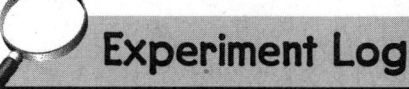

4. What is one thing you will change in your test?

5. What things will you need for your test? Write or draw them here.

6. What steps will you take to do your test?

Name _____

Do the test.

7. Record your data in the chart.

How Does the Sun's Heat Change Water?

Morning Temperature	Noon Temperature	Afternoon Temperature

Draw conclusions. Communicate results.

8. What are your results? How can you communicate your results to others?

_____
_____
_____
_____
_____

Name _____

Unit E Experiment Log

Solids in Water

Observe and ask a question.

1. What can you ask about the way that solids dissolve in water of different temperatures?

_____
- -
_____

Form a hypothesis.

2. What could be true about how water temperature changes the way salt and sugar dissolve?

_____
- -
_____

Plan a fair test.

3. What things will you keep the same in the test? Write or draw them here.

Name _____ Experiment Log

4. What is one thing you will change in the test?

5. What objects will you need to do the test? Write or draw them here.

6. What steps will you take to do the test?

Name _____   **Experiment Log**

Do the test.

7. Record your data in the chart.

How Does Water Temperature Change the Way Solids Dissolve?

Name of Solid	Cold Water	Hot Water
	Dissolving time: _____ seconds	Dissolving time: _____ seconds
	Dissolving time: _____ seconds	Dissolving time: _____ seconds

Draw conclusions. Communicate results.

8. What are your results? How can you communicate your results to others?

_____
_____
_____
_____

Use with page E1.   (page 3 of 3)   Workbook • WB177

Name _____

**Unit F
Experiment Log**

Height and Distance

Observe and ask a question.

1. What can you ask about the way height affects distance?

_____
_____

Form a hypothesis.

2. What could be true about the way a change in height changes the distance a toy truck will go?

_____
_____

Plan a fair test.

3. What things will you keep the same in the test? Write or draw them here.

WB178 • Workbook (page 1 of 3) Use with page F1.

Name _____ Experiment Log

4. What is one thing you will change in the test?

5. What objects will you need to do the test? Write or draw them here.

6. What steps will you take to do the test?

Name _____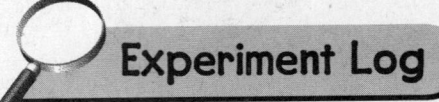

Do the test.

7. Record your data in the chart.

How Does the Height of a Ramp Change How Far a Toy Truck Will Go?

Height of Ramp (Board)	Distance the Truck Rolls

Draw conclusions. Communicate results.

8. What are your results? How can you communicate your results to others?

_____
_____
_____
_____
_____
_____